"Wow. The moment I read the first page, I was crying. I couldn't put the book down. I have a little boy who just turned four, and can't imagine ever leaving him for longer than I have to. All I wanted to do was grab my little boy out of his bed and hold him. I am deeply humbled by this story. I hope it will change the lives of millions of people. It has mine."

—Brian Littrell
Recording artist
Member of the Backstreet Boys

"*Castaway Kid* is an awesome story of the power of Jesus to redeem every facet of our lives. This is a great book that reminds me personally of God's love. I cried real tears reading this; it is a must read."

—Dave Ramsey
New York Times bestselling author
The Total Money Makeover

"Before you sit down to read *Castaway Kid* by Rob Mitchell, I would suggest that you obtain a box of tissues. This compelling story grabs from the first page and helps you to understand what real loneliness and rejection feel like. More importantly, it puts into perspective the most important things in life, such as a relationship with God. This is a splendid example of how the hand of God can heal all wounds and boost us toward the goal of realizing our innate potential. When you finish this book, you will be ready to put down the tissue and pick up your conqueror's helmet."

—Benjamin S. Carson, Sr., M.D.
Johns Hopkins Medical Institutions
Author, *Gifted Hands: The Ben Carson Story*

"A powerful, compelling message that points to the unimaginable grace of our heavenly Father."

—Dan T. Cathy
President and chief operating officer
Chick-fil-A, Inc.

"In an era espousing 'self-esteem,' Rob Mitchell points out with actual experience how badly all of us need God's help in our lives and endeavors. An important read!"

—Ben Edwards
Retired chairman
A.G. Edwards & Sons, Inc.

"This is a remarkable work of contemporary literature that quickly gets inside the reader's head, then heart. The book starts out as a little boy's struggle with abandonment but quickly becomes the reader's own struggle with universal themes of loneliness, fear, rejection, anger, bitterness, and how to forgive others and ourselves."

—Dotty Hoots
English educator, Wesleyan Academy
High Point, North Carolina

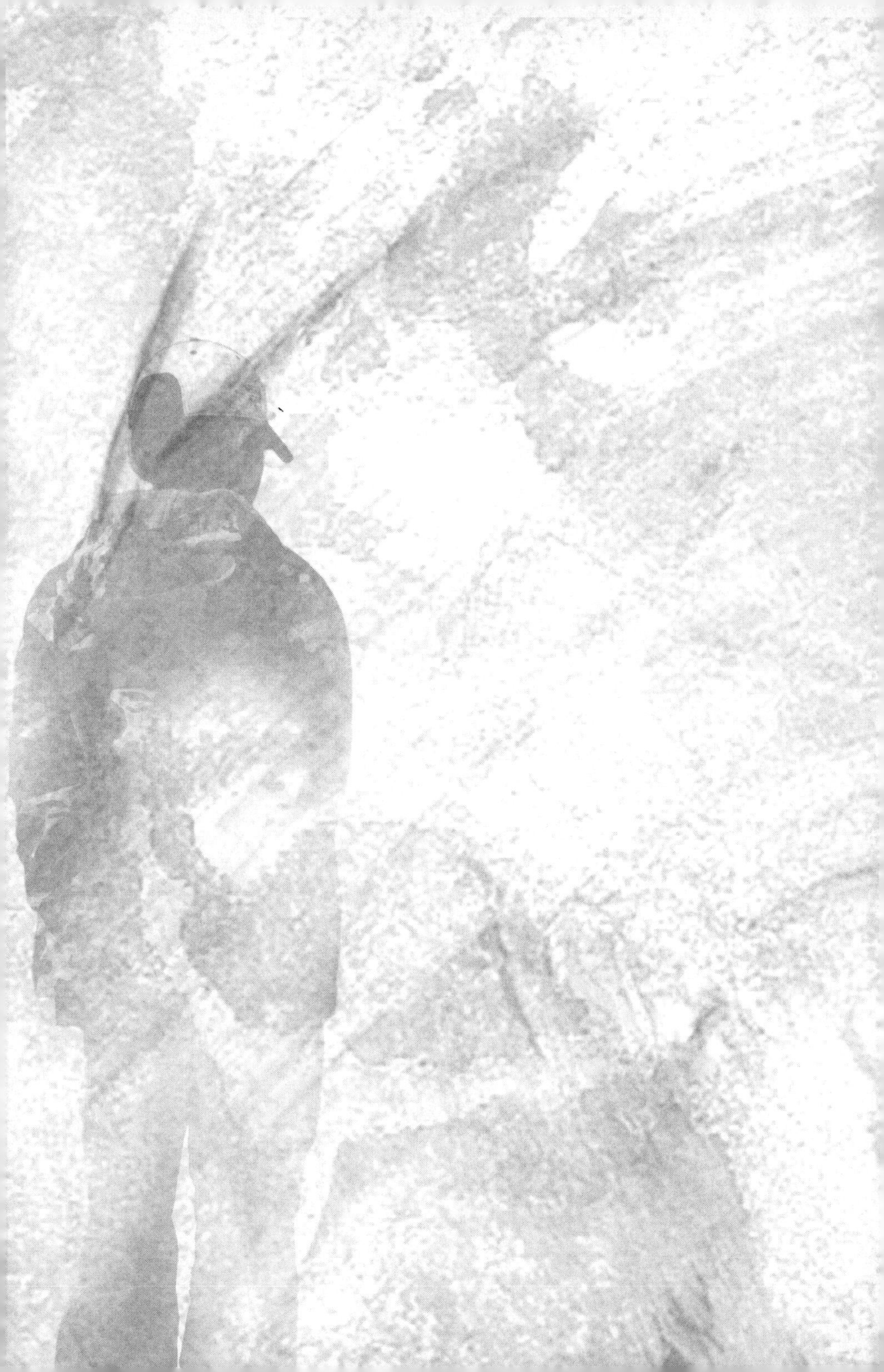

FOCUS ON THE FAMILY®

r. b. mitchell

Castaway Kid

Tyndale House Publishers, Inc.
Carol Stream, Illinois

A Focus on the Family book published by Tyndale House Publishers, Carol Stream, Illinois 60188

Photo illustration: Joseph Sapulich
Model: Joshua Sapulich

Library of Congress Cataloging-in-Publication Data
Mitchell, R. B. (Robert Bivings), 1954-
Castaway kid : one man's search for hope and home / R.B. Mitchell.
p. cm. — (Focus on the family)
ISBN-13: 978-1-58997-434-0
ISBN-10: 1-58997-434-4
1. Mitchell, R. B. (Robert Bivings), 1954- 2. Orphans—Illinois—Biography. 3. Children—Institutional Care—Illinois—Case studies. 4. Parental rejection—Illinois—Case studies. 5. Adult children of dysfunctional families—Biography. I. Title.
HV990.I36M57 2007
362.73092—dc22
[B]

2006035652

Printed in the United States of America
5 6 7 8 9 / 12 11 10 09 08

To the lonely who have wounded themselves or
been wounded by the abuse or apathy of others—
and
to those who pray without ceasing,
trying to bring hope.

Contents

Acknowledgments

God, who leads beyond imagination if I listen.

Susan, my wife and helpmate: Your outer beauty is overshadowed by your intelligent, sensitive, and caring inner beauty, which has strengthened me on our journey together.

Alicia and Luke: Being your father has been the joy of my life.

Paul: Once only a sojourner, now a brother.

My Rockford folks: Art, Paul, Marge, and "the girls."

Joe and Mary Davis, deceased: Susan's parents and wonderful in-laws.

Also, thank you to . . .

Those in Princeton not listed in the book, but who tried: Carol, Colleen, George, Helen, John, Ralph, and Tim, as well as the Swanson and Malm families.

Those in college: the Eds, Barbie, David, Doug, Gerry, Jimmy, John, Kate, and the New Garden youth group.

Missionaries Ruth and Brad Hill, and Jan and Bob Thornbloom. *Mbote!*

The men who keep me accountable: Barry, Jay, Pete, and Steve.

The men of CBMC, especially Pat O'Neal.

The Cathys of Chick-fil-A and their at-risk kids' organization, WinShape.

Kiwanis members who reach out to at-risk kids and invite me to help.

The Red Pen Partners of Massachusetts.

Dotty Hoots and her students in Wesleyan Academy class of '04, the best.

Phil Downer of DNA Ministries, and our buddy, Ken Walker, for encouragement.

Ronda, Ruth, and Vivien, who keep things running.

Nanci and John, my guides at Focus.

And Barbara Winslow Robidoux, my writing coach who became my friend.

Is This Story True?

THIS IS A BOOK OF HOPE. Even so, with recent furors over memoirs that have contained questionable "facts," it's valid to ask whether this really is a true story.

Speaking at a fundraiser for the Covenant Children's Home in the early 1990s, I learned from the director that having never been a ward of the state, I had full access to my caseworker files. I tagged a number of documents for my records, often thinking, *If you ever wrote a book, people would think you made this up.*

But all the events occurred. They've been recalled not only as faithfully as I can remember, but also as other adults involved have remembered and documented in caseworker notes, recorded interviews, and my grandmother Gigi's journal.

So they can tell their own stories when and if they choose, other kids from the orphanage are not named—except one, and with permission. No names in the book are made up, though a few are nicknames.

I've been told I have an unusually accurate memory. No one's recollection is perfect, of course, but the dialogue in this book is in keeping with the essence of each situation and as close to word-for-word as possible. All the living adults who are quoted and whom I've been able to reach have confirmed my memories of the events in which they were involved.

Yes, this story of hope is true. You can find further details on the Web at www.amillionlittleproofs.com.

"Character,
not circumstances,
makes the man."

—Booker T. Washington
Slave turned educator

1

Cast Away

DIM, FUZZY IMAGES FORM MOST of my early childhood memories. But one is clear and sharp.

Fear burned it permanently on my three-year-old brain.

Mother and I are standing in front of a large building. Piles of snow line the sidewalk.

"C'mon, Robby," Mother says as she drags me up the steps to the front door. "They're waiting for us."

Soon we're staying in a strange bedroom. I don't know why. Eerie sounds and shadows keep me whimpering when I wake during the night. Mother shushes me.

A loud bell rings and wakes us up. The sun is shining and the scary shadows have disappeared. Unfamiliar sounds from last night change to running feet and laughter.

We eat breakfast in a big room with lots of kids, but they don't seem to see us. When we finish, Mother takes me upstairs. A nameless lady in a long, dark dress meets us.

"Why don't you go over there and play?" she says, pointing to a corner where a boy stacks building blocks.

I don't move.

"Do what she says, Robby!" Mother orders.

Clinging to Mother's leg, I hesitate. She brushes my hand away, grabs my arm, and drags me to the play area. She plops me on the floor, facing the boy with my back to her.

I reach for a block, but the kid grabs it. When he begins to scoop the other toys away from me, I turn to complain.

Only the strange lady is standing there.

Mother is gone.

"Mommy had to go to the hospital, Robby," the woman tells me. "She took the train back to Chicago. She'll come to see you again when she gets better."

Her mouth keeps moving, but I don't hear the words. When it finally sinks in that Mother has left me, I begin to whimper.

"Stop that, Robby," the woman commands. "Play with the toys."

"I want Mommy!" I scream. "I want Daddy. I want Grandma Gigi. I wanna go home!" The screams turn to loud sobs as I run toward the door. I try to open it, but can't turn the handle.

"Stop that crying, Robby, or I'm going to spank you!" the woman warns.

"I wanna go home! I wanna go home!" I cry, throwing myself on the floor and kicking my feet.

The tantrum pushes her to the end of her patience. Yanking me off the floor, she spanks me again and again. Finally I clamp my teeth together to keep the cries inside.

She stops, but I can't quit sniffling.

That night, the other kids ignore me.

When morning comes, I wake up in a wet bed. The woman scolds me.

After breakfast she puts a brown rubber cover over the mattress and a brown rubber sheet on top. She makes me lie between them all morning.

The rubber sheets are hot. They squeak when I move.

"Pee-pee baby," some of the boys chant. "New kid is a pee-pee baby." I'm ashamed, but too afraid to say anything.

The squeak of brown rubber sheets has tagged me as being bad, different.

Different from the other boys at the place where Mother has abandoned me.

In the weeks and months that followed, I heard nothing from Mother. But I did hear from Grandma Gigi.

I don't know how or when she found out where I was. But once she did, she took the train from Chicago every Saturday to visit me in the little farming town of Princeton, Illinois.

Gigi was in her 60s, divorced, and poor. Living alone in a tiny apartment, she worked as a clerk at the big Marshall Field's department store downtown. My mother, Joyce Mitchell, was her only child; I was Gigi's only grandchild.

Visiting me wasn't easy for Gigi. It meant leaving her apartment on the north side of the city early in the morning, walking four blocks on Ridge Boulevard to Howard Street, and catching a bus to the Howard station—then taking the Red Line elevated train to Belmont, changing to the Purple Line to Adams and Quincy, and walking several long blocks to Union Station. There she caught the train known as the California Zephyr and rode for two hours to Princeton. Arriving about 10 A.M., she'd face five more blocks to the Covenant Children's Home.

When she finally saw me, Gigi would kneel and wait for me to run to her. Somehow she stayed on her feet as I threw myself into her arms. Hugging me close, she smelled good. She always looked like a lady—a modest but flattering dress covering her medium build, along with earrings, a necklace, nylon stockings, heels, and a hat with short, dark curls peeking out from under the brim.

"What new things have you learned since last I was here?" she'd always ask. I'd tell her all I could think of, then proudly tug her to the playground to show her my latest trick.

I was proud, too, when she said "Hi" to some of the other boys and called them by name. Kids like us felt special when someone remembered who we were.

Toward noon Gigi and I would walk to a small restaurant nearby. She ordered coffee, but rarely ate a meal. She let me look at the menu, then said, "How about a hamburger and a nice glass of milk? We'll have ice cream for dessert." That always sounded good to me.

But 2:00 P.M. would come much too soon. Gigi had to say good-bye and leave to catch the 3:00 train back to the city.

"Gigi, take me with you," I would beg. "Please, Gigi, please take me with you!"

That's when she would kneel again, tears in her eyes, saying the same thing she always said. "Robby, darling, you're my precious grandson. I'm sorry I can't keep you with me. I'm sorry your parents are too sick to keep you. Keep my love in your heart. It will always be there."

I didn't understand what she meant. All I knew was that love seemed to fill me up each Saturday when she was with me. When she left, I felt empty and alone.

Time after time, standing outside the front door of the Children's Home, I watched her walk away. Arms crossed and hands tucked into armpits, I rocked slightly left to right.

Why won't you take me home with you? I cried silently. *I'll be a good boy, Gigi. I promise. I won't eat much! Please, please don't leave me here.*

Finally she would disappear from my tear-blurred sight.

And the only one left to hug me was . . . me.

/2/

Little Boys

It's not clear how many months passed before my bed-wetting stopped, but the rubber sheets came off shortly before Nola arrived. Twenty-nine years old and never married, our new houseparent was a no-nonsense woman with a big smile and sparkling eyes.

She usually dressed in long, plain dresses or a blouse and pedal pusher pants, cat-eyes glasses, and no jewelry, and always kept her wavy, dark hair cut short. When asked why, Nola laughed and said, "Don't have time to fuss with my hair and a dozen wild young'uns!" I fell in love with her!

Nola was quick to laugh and quick to hug. She spanked us when we needed it, but only for a good reason and with love. Her consistent warmth helped fill some of the emptiness in my heart.

That let me concentrate on getting to know my new surroundings.

The Covenant Children's Home sat on a 20-acre triangle at the northeastern edge of Princeton. Fields of corn and soybeans lined one edge of the property, open pasture the other.

A main building contained dormitory units, staff offices, a dining hall, and a visitor's lounge. A smaller structure housed a laundry upstairs and a boiler room downstairs. A barn, a chicken coop, and vegetable gardens were located further away.

Safely back from Elm Street was our giant play area. There were big swing sets, a merry-go-round, tether ball, a basketball court, slides, and a baseball field. I was fascinated by the enormous, fire-engine-red playset with gymnastic rings, chin-up bar, sliding poles, and tall ladders. But I wasn't brave enough yet to climb that high.

There were four units: Little Boys, Little Girls, Big Boys, Big Girls. The smaller building's second floor housed Big Boys; in the main building, Big Girls and Little Girls shared the third floor while Little Boys filled the second floor.

Eight to sixteen boys under age ten lived in our Little Boys unit. Nola lived with us on the unit and had a small private bedroom and bath.

There was nothing private about our bathroom. There were two of everything, and everything was white—white-painted wooden stalls for the white toilets, white ceramic-tiled floor, white cast-iron tubs, and white sinks low to the floor for easy reaching.

We had a large living room with industrial-strength carpet, two long, heavy-duty couches, a couple of rugged chairs, and a pair of large tables for homework, drawing, and games. The brown TV, bigger than I was, had a rabbit-ears antenna to receive the few stations we could bring in.

In our four bedrooms, black cast-iron single beds sat on black linoleum floors. One room had three beds, one five; the other two had four.

An oak chest with several drawers completed each room. Every kid had a drawer he called his own, assigned according to height. My drawer was the bottom one; at three, I was the shortest.

That drawer, I learned, was reserved for hidden treasures. Even peeking into another boy's drawer meant getting the fool beat out of you by everyone else in the room. My drawer mostly contained pretty rocks and feathers I found on the playground. I'd look at them at least once a day just to make sure they were still there. Some kids never opened theirs.

Keeping track of people was harder. Since kids frequently came and went, there was little time to make friends. Some stayed for only a day or two. Others were there for a few months or longer. Kids often arrived angry, confused, and frustrated.

It didn't help to be part of a crowd. We lived with many others, but each of us felt alone.

The staff tried to deal with our wide range of backgrounds and emotions. To help keep order, strict rules were enforced and a regular daily routine was followed.

In the early mornings, for example, no one was allowed out of bed until a bell rang. We could sit up. We could talk. We could dangle our legs over the side of the bed. But we could not put a foot on the floor. We got in trouble if Nola walked by one of our rooms and saw even a toe on the floor before the bell rang.

At precisely 7:00 A.M., the bell clanged and the entire unit went into action. We hopped out of our beds and quickly made them to Nola's satisfaction. Then we ran to the bathroom, where the shared toilets led to plenty of waiting and squirming.

We brushed our teeth and washed our faces with two or more to a sink, then hurried to get dressed. It was a wild scene as eight to sixteen boys stampeded into the locker room and scrambled to put on the day's outfit that Nola had laid out on the floor in front of each locker.

Our lockers didn't have doors, just wooden sides built into the wall and painted a color that reminded me of split pea soup. Wide and deep, they allowed us to climb in and hide behind clothes. The bottom was off the floor for some reason; that's where our one or two pairs of shoes went. Since many kids showed up with just the clothes on their backs, few had their own hanging in there.

Most of our clothes were hand-me-downs from local folks whose kids had outgrown them, or gifts from clothing stores or church groups. Little Boys shirts seemed to be either plaid flannels or plain white T-shirts. Pants rarely fit, so more than half the time we wore suspenders to keep them up. Nola rolled up too-long pants legs for each of us.

Once we were finally dressed, punching and pushing like a ragtag army, we lined up behind Nola and marched downstairs to the dining hall for breakfast—which was always served at 7:30. Eating at the Home was a task, not a social event. Most of us shoveled the meal down in five minutes. For reasons never made clear, we were required to sit at the table for at least ten.

After breakfast, the junior and senior high kids were driven to the public schools in Princeton on an ugly yellow bus with embarrassingly large letters proclaiming COVENANT CHILDREN'S HOME. Douglas Elementary was only two blocks away, so some of the staff walked younger kids there and back.

As the youngest child the Home had accepted in a long time, I usually was the only kid not in school. I loved having Nola to myself. Following her around like a bouncing, blond puppy, I helped her sort dirty clothes to take to the laundry. She'd put a few garments in a pillowcase, and I'd proudly carry or drag them down the stairs, out the door, across the basketball court, and up another set of stairs to the laundry with its big washers and dryers.

To keep me off the lint-covered floor and out of trouble, Nola plopped me on top of a table where I could watch the laundry staff washing clothes and sheets for the 60 kids and staff. There were always women volunteers from the local Covenant church; they called themselves "Covy" women. I saw them pull armfuls of hot clothes and sheets from dryers, then load wheeled laundry baskets and push them to long tables where sorting and folding took place.

Houseparents didn't do laundry, but Nola insisted on ironing our Sunday dress shirts. When another staff person asked why Nola didn't let a "laundry lady" do it, she gave a no-nonsense reply: "I don't mind. Some of the boys are allergic to starch and others like a lot, so I give them each what they like. It's no trouble, and they need a few special touches in their little lives."

On days when the laundry ladies were in a good mood, and after most of the work was done, I waited until Nola wasn't looking—and dove headfirst into a basket of fresh, warm sheets.

"Where are you, Robby?" she would fuss playfully. "Where have you gone? Oh, dear me, where is that boy?" She'd stick her hands into the pile of sheets and make a show of searching, the laundry jiggling as I tried to stifle my giggles.

Finally she'd grab my ankles and pull me out feetfirst, head down, squealing like a happy piglet. "There you are, child," she'd chuckle with fake joy. "I didn't think I'd ever find you!"

Nola was no longer just mine, though, when the other boys returned from school. Slam-banging in, they dropped their books and sat for a cookies-and-juice snack. Some boys played and some did chores as Nola reviewed homework assignments and notes from teachers. The latter usually led her to scold one or two kids who'd talked back to a teacher or fought on the school playground.

At 5:00 P.M. we washed our faces and hands, then marched to the dining hall. Standing on the alternating black and red linoleum squares, about sixty kids and six adults prayed as we did before every meal: "God is great; God is good. Let us thank Him for our food. Amen." The chorus was loud, but the tone was a singsong "We've done this a thousand times before."

Noise and confusion followed. Boys elbowed other boys or made faces at the girls. Chairs scraped. It was all I could do to maneuver my heavy oak chair far enough from the table to climb into, only to get stuck. Frustrated and embarrassed because I was too small to get my seat close enough to the table, I waited each time as Nola came over to push my chair in for me.

I couldn't wait to grow big enough to do it myself. Or, better yet, to do what the Big Boys did—swing a leg over the back of the chair and plop like a cowboy mounting a horse.

After supper, the routine continued. Older boys went to their rooms to do homework while Nola got us younger ones ready for bed. If it was Wednesday or Saturday night, baths were in order. We grumbled; for us, a bath twice a week was at least once a week too often.

Complaining never did us any good, though; Nola had a mission. With only two tubs for her squirming herd, she tried to get six of us clean before changing the water. That meant two of us in one tub. The first pair got clean, the second lost a little dirt, and the third just had fun.

By 7:00 P.M. we were in our pajamas, and Nola gathered us into the living room like a mother hen with her chicks. It was Bible story time.

Sitting in the middle of the heavy oak couch in the corner, Nola would put her arm around me as she invited the youngest boys to join her. The older ones settled on the floor, sitting with crossed legs or stretching out on their stomachs. Nola demanded quiet attention—no talking or goofing off. I didn't know much about the Bible, but I knew this was a special time.

Then off to bed. Nola always knelt at each bedside, whispered a prayer that only that boy heard, kissed him "good night," and told him she loved him.

Once, when I woke up and padded down the hall to use the bathroom, the door to Nola's little bedroom was open. I vaguely heard her praying, using boys' names. As I padded back down the hall, she hollered, "Flush the toilet, Robby!"

I never understood how she recognized the way each of us walked.

Passing her door for the second time, I stopped and knocked.

Nola came to the door in her plain, pink flannel gown. "Yes?" she said.

"Whatcha praying about?" I asked. "That we behave?"

"No, Robby," she answered matter-of-factly. "I pray God helps me find something to love in each of you."

I didn't know what to say to that.

Before I could think of a reply, she picked me up and squeezed me tight. Carrying me back to bed she playfully whispered, "Although *you* might need some *extra* prayer to behave!"

As winter came again, Gigi continued her weekly visits. Nola's caring attention never failed.

But the loneliness remained.

I knew little about "normal" kids, but I longed to leave the Home and have a home and family of my own.

A year was stretching into two. Still I heard nothing from Mother; by now she was little more than a memory.

But then, suddenly, things changed. The woman who had left me with strangers was back, bringing chaos.

/3/

The Tornado

IT WAS 1959, NEARLY TWO years after my mother had abandoned me. I was five years old.

One day, without explanation, Nola took me downstairs to the visitor's room.

Mother was standing there.

Running to her, I threw my arms around her leg. *I'm going home,* I told myself. *Mommy's out of the hospital and here to take me home. I'm going home!*

"Hello, Robby," she said without much feeling. "How are you doing?"

I didn't know how to answer that.

She didn't kneel and hug me like Gigi did, so I grabbed her hand. "C'mon to the playground like Gigi does, Mommy. I'll show you all the tricks I learned on the swings and monkey bars."

"That's not important, Robby!" she said coldly. "We have more important things to talk about!"

Feeling like a puppy that's just been kicked, I dropped her hand, hung my head, and shut my mouth.

"We'll be going to town for lunch," Mother declared. Grabbing my hand, she headed for the door. Walking faster than I could, she jerked me forward to keep up.

We left the grounds and walked several blocks to a restaurant. She rambled on about things I didn't understand: "Too many immigrants here. Should send the blacks back to the South. Let your witch of a grandmother Pauline deal with them in Atlanta. She's destroyed my life by messing up your father. She never gave him the freedom he needed, and he wasn't man enough to stand up to her!"

We didn't stop until she found a restaurant that served beer. People smoked and played pool there, too.

When we returned, reeking of smoke, the Swedish Christians who ran the Home were not happy. Nola kept her voice calm, but clearly was upset. Through gritted teeth she said, "That restaurant is not appropriate for a young child, Mrs. Mitchell. Please choose the one closer to campus. It has a nice family atmosphere. Or you could stay on campus and join us all in the dining hall."

"I'm his mother, and I know what's best for him," she fired back. Then she launched into a list of demands. "Give him special pillows. No wool blankets. Feed him the diet I've written out on this paper."

Nola shook her head, then nodded, silently taking it all in.

"When he begins kindergarten, have a taxi take him back and forth to school. No sports." She reached into her pocket and pulled out another sheet of paper. "And here's some Bible verses I want him to memorize by the time I come back!"

When are we going home? I thought. *Stop talking to Nola and let's go. We can take the train Gigi takes.*

But without warning, Mother turned to me and announced, "Gotta go!"

Offering no hug or kiss, she turned away and walked swiftly down the front walk, strode off the property, and headed toward the train station.

You're leaving without me? Again?

No words or tears would come.

Stunned, I looked up at Nola. Gently she reached down and took my hand, and we walked wordlessly back into the Home.

For days I didn't talk or play. I wandered to a far section of the playground, where I stared into space and wondered how long my mother would act this way.

The other kids didn't bother me. Kids like us seemed to understand when someone needed to be left alone.

It was not the last time Mother would make a surprise appearance. Over the next couple of years, she repeated these scenes again and again.

Her erratic visits were tornado-like events. Since she didn't call ahead to let anyone know she was coming, it sometimes took Nola time to get me to the visitor's lounge. When we arrived, Mother would scream accusations at Nola, charging her and the rest of the Home staff with hiding her son from his mother.

During these rants my heart went cold as Mother ignored me. Then she'd drag me to the same lunch at the same pool hall with the same lecture routine.

Each time, she would leave me behind.

Maybe this time will be different, I kept telling myself. *Maybe she won't be angry and yell at Nola. Maybe she'll have a good job so she can take me home with her. Maybe we can be a family again.*

Each visit I was disappointed. I would spend days trying to deal with the pain.

My staff social worker spent more time with me now. He tried to get me to tell him or Nola what I was thinking and feeling. All I could say was, "My heart hurts. It hurts bad."

Soon I stopped calling my mother "Mommy."

It wasn't an easy thing to do. I wanted this woman to love me. But I thought "Mommy" was what you called a woman who tucked you into bed at night, who kept you safe and took good care of you. Mommy was someone you were proud of.

My mother was never a mommy to me.

"Why isn't she like other mothers?" I sometimes asked Nola. "Why does she yell and cuss at you? That's not nice!"

Nola said little, but I kept asking anyway.

"Why does she smell so bad? Do I have to go to lunch with her? She smokes cigarettes, drinks coffee, and goes on and on about stuff I don't understand."

Nola listened and nodded, letting me get it all out.

"She doesn't watch me play like you and Gigi do, Nola. Doesn't she like me?"

When Nola figured I'd let off enough steam, she'd say softly, "She's sick, Robby. It's not your fault that you have to live here. You're not the problem."

"Sick from what? Why can't the doctors make her better? What's wrong with her?"

Nola never answered that question, either.

But sometimes she knelt down, pulled me into her arms, and held me tight. "You're safe here, Robby," she'd whisper. "Remember that I love you and God loves you, too."

Burying my head against her shoulder and snuggling into the safety of her arms, I wondered: *Why didn't God make my mother more like Nola?*

/9/

Different

STARTING KINDERGARTEN TOOK ME OUT of Nola's nest for a few hours each weekday morning. Strutting the two-block walk to Douglas Elementary was a big deal, making me feel really grown up.

The other kids in my class were friendly, and as innocent as I was. There were plenty of fun things to report and papers to show each time Gigi came to visit. She seemed as excited as I was over the things I was learning. In the evenings, Nola gave me "pretend homework" so I could feel like one of the gang.

But then came first grade, and another innocence was dashed.

I hadn't realized that coming from the Home made me different. But things changed when I saw some mean boys from the upper grades surround and taunt another kid from the Home.

The boy cried.

The mean boys laughed.

I stared.

Elementary schoolyard bullies seemed to know just what to say, which button to push, to get one of us "Homies" to cry or lash back. We were easy targets.

Eventually they got to me, too. My hot button was, "What's wrong with you, Robby? Why you got no parents?"

"I do too have parents," I protested. "They just can't take care of me right now. But we're gonna be a family again real soon."

"Yeah, sure! You're stupid or a liar. Your folks just don't want you."

The first time it happened, I burst into tears. The bullies laughed. Other kids kept quiet.

When I complained to Nola that night, she said, "Don't let them know it bothers you, Robby. Just say 'Sticks and stones may break my bones, but words will never hurt me,' then walk away from them."

That sounded like a good plan—until I tried it a few times. The bullies' laughter just made me feel worse. Sticks and stones would have been easier to handle.

Each week the Townies' taunts increased my pain. But then came the day in second grade when I'd had enough.

It happened quickly, surprising me almost as much as it did the bully. A jeer was hardly out of the other boy's mouth before my fists were flying. It felt good to beat the fool out of him.

Fighting was nothing new to me by this time. The older boys at the Home had taught me well—painfully well. I knew where to hit to keep from leaving telltale bruises and bumps, just how to punch the ribs and skull to leave the longest-lasting aches.

My suddenly violent responses and tough attitude stopped many verbal attacks after that. But there was always some kid who set me off, buying me a ticket to the principal's office. When I got there, the frowning principal would ask, "What's wrong with you, boy?"

What's wrong with me? What's wrong with you, *Mr. Principal? It's not me; the other kid started it! I didn't know there was anything wrong with me until I came here!*

When the man asked that question, I wanted to smash him. I had no answer. Retreating into a cave of sullen resignation, I waited for the punishment that followed. If he was looking for signs of regret, he never saw them.

A caseworker at the Home began to spend time talking with me each week. He tried to help me get past the feelings of being singled out at school. But no matter how often he and Nola told me I was okay, I couldn't believe it.

Bad stuff is always happening to me, and I don't know why, I thought. *No one wants me—not even the kids from town. No matter what Nola says, I must be bad! I wish someone would tell me what I did wrong. Why did Mother send me away? Why am I so alone?*

Sure, I still lived in a herd of 60 kids. But in my heart, I was still alone—desperately alone.

No father was teaching me "guy stuff." No big brother was protecting me from the teenagers that rapped us younger ones in the head with their knuckles. No mother wanted to kiss my hurts and tuck me in at night.

It must be my fault. There had to be something wrong with me. *I must be too hard to live with.* The trouble I got into confirmed those feelings. *I must be the bad one in our family.*

I wasn't the only kid at the home who felt that way about himself. Watching the others, I slowly began to realize that all of us wanted to believe our parents were the best in the world. Unless they'd been severely abused, the kids I knew refused to agree that their parents were the problem.

It was easier if things were our fault. If we were the problem, we could try hard to be good and change ourselves. Then our parents would want to take us back home.

The social workers gently tried to get us to accept the idea that our parents were the problem. But if that was true, it might be a long time before they got better and we could go home. If our parents couldn't get fixed, we'd never leave.

It wasn't that things were so bad at the Home that we hated it. Most of us got much better care there than our parents had given us. But even at age seven I could see that kids preferred poverty if they were loved, rags if they were cared for, and homelessness if someone wanted them. We were willing to suffer much if we could only be part of our own families.

I saw it in kids at the Home who came from a family of 11, whose father worked only part-time jobs and lived in a makeshift shack near the town dump. The kids were hungry, wore dirty clothes, and looked like they never bathed. Adults called the father a bum. Physically they were better off at the Home, but for at least the first couple of years they resented not being at their family's shack.

I saw it in a girl who came to the Home after her mother died of cancer. Her father couldn't handle his wife's death and couldn't deal with his only child. She lost not only her mother but also the father she needed to help her through the grief. Despite her father's rejection, she still hoped to return to him and to what home meant.

I saw it in a boy at the home whose brain seemed not to work as fast as most. His father regularly beat him for being "stupid," while his mother ignored him and focused on her "normal" kids. For years this boy wanted to go home, desperately hoping things would be different and his own family would accept him.

We all wanted to believe it. We all wanted to think that soon we would get to live our dream of going to a home where we were wanted and loved.

The older kids seemed to give up that dream eventually, reaching a silent acceptance of their lot in life. But for us younger ones, it was more difficult. Every one of us on Little Boys believed that if we could somehow get back home, the dark shadow of loneliness would go away.

That shadow didn't make me cry out loud anymore. But it still haunted me. In bed with the lights out, I often quietly let the tears flow.

When that happened, I told myself that somehow, someday, in some mysterious way, things would get better and I'd be rescued. That hope was the only thing that kept despair from dragging me into its dark pit.

That and Gigi. She was a blessing many of the other kids at the Home didn't have. I looked forward to her visits, which always warmed my heart.

At Christmas, and occasionally Thanksgiving, I was allowed to go to Gigi's apartment. On one of those visits I met her relatives from Rockford, Illinois. Fran was the daughter of Gigi's oldest brother. She and her sons, Paul and Art, were nice and invited me to visit them.

The first time I met them, I was so happy my mind went into overdrive. *Maybe I can live with them!*

The thought had no sooner entered my brain before I blurted out, "Can I maybe come and live with you? I do good in school and I know how to do chores. I'll be a lot of help if you let me come."

Gigi was astonished, but Fran was gentle. "I'm so sorry, Robby.

But I'm nearly 70 and too old to take care of you. Art is single and travels a lot on business. Paul already has four daughters. So as much as we'd like to help, there's no way we can take you home with us."

I could sense that she and her family liked me. But it felt as if another door had just slammed in my face.

Nobody seemed to understand that I was haunted by a question: *Why? Why isn't any family member willing to take me in and raise me?*

I struggled to keep hope alive. But in the winter of second grade I lost that battle.

It was February, 1962. I was seven years old.

The central Illinois farmland was stark and barren that night. Fields of cornstalks and soybean plants had been plowed under. Dirty snow covered dead grass; trees naked of leaves creaked in bitter winds.

Nola had put us to bed, leaving us alone with our thoughts. Weird shadows from the bathroom nightlight and the red light from the EXIT sign slithered across the bedroom walls. In my four years at the Home, such spooky nights had fueled many bad dreams.

As I lay in bed, I finally had to admit the truth.

My father was not going to get well.

My mother would never be like other mothers.

I wouldn't ever be able to live with Gigi or her relatives.

No one was going to rescue me.

Reality crushed my heart.

Sobs gushed forth from a soft place I thought I'd shielded. I'd heard such anguished cries from other boys when they lost hope, but somehow I had managed to avoid falling into such despair.

Not tonight. Tonight it was my turn to cry out with groanings too deep for words.

"Shut up!" the boys who shared the bedroom barked at me. My raw emotion threatened the defenses they'd built around their own wounded, fearful hearts.

Nola came and held me. But she couldn't stay long. Soon she had to tend to a younger child.

I cried until there were no tears left. Exhausted and smothered in grief, I reflected long into the night.

No one's going to rescue me. No one is ever going to rescue me.

I'm alone and I don't know why. What did I do wrong? I was only three when she left me here. What could I possibly have done to deserve this?

I don't understand, and I can't escape. I'm stuck here forever—I'm here, like it or not.

On that cold winter night, I hardened my heart.

Nothing and nobody will hurt me this badly again. The big boys can beat me until I cry with pain, but no one is ever going to make me cry from my heart like this again. No one! I'm going to be tough—no matter what!

It was only a little boy's vow.

But it was all I had to protect me from the living nightmare that lurked around the corner.

/5/

Kidnapped

JANUARY 19, 1963, 8:15 P.M.

According to caseworker notes, Mother showed up unexpectedly at the Home, demanding to see me.

She was taking me with her, she told Nola. Since Mother had legal custody, no one could stop her.

"Mrs. Mitchell, it's bedtime for our eight-year-olds—and it's dangerously cold out tonight," Nola said sternly. "When can we expect Robby back?"

Mother laughed, swore at Nola, and dragged me off.

Afraid and confused, I looked back to Nola for help. She resembled an angry, trembling she-wolf straining at the end of her chain.

Mother was wild as we walked toward town. She ranted and cussed with more passion than ever, but smirked as if playing some game.

She jerked me often because I didn't walk as fast as she did. I was cold, but didn't dare to complain.

As usual, she griped about my grandmothers, the Home, the Bible, blacks, and immigrants. But then she said something new.

"I'm going to show them, Robby. I'm going to show them all. They'll see I can be a good mother. Soon our family will be together again."

Home? Am I finally going home? I knew better than to ask that out loud. Like a frightened puppy, I watched and waited.

We didn't return to the Home that night. Instead, Mother sneaked us in to sleep on the cold, wooden benches in the little Princeton train station.

Next morning we took the first train to Chicago. When I told her I had no extra clothes, she said, "Don't you worry, Robby. I've got it all taken care of."

Arriving in Chicago, we went straight to the world-famous Palmer House Hotel. The leap from cast-iron orphanage beds to sparkling chandeliers, spacious rooms, and sharply dressed bellhops seemed like a dream. It was a world more beautiful than I'd ever imagined.

After we settled in a room, Mother pulled a bunch of money out of her bigger-than-usual pocketbook. "I finally got what's owed me," she said, stuffing the bills into a dresser drawer. "My father and his sister got killed when a train hit their car. I got $10,000 from his life insurance! Isn't that great?"

I didn't know how to answer that.

"This drawer is yours," she announced with pride. "Come see what I bought you."

Comic books! The drawer was stuffed with them. Mother had told me many times that comic books were evil; now she laughed when she saw my dazed expression. Later in the week she lectured me again about how bad comic books were—then went out and bought me a dozen more.

For a few weeks, life was a fantasy come true. We ordered food from room service. We shopped at fancy department stores. We saw one movie after another.

The rants, however, continued. Mother raved about how Grandmother Pauline, my father's mother, had snatched this kind of lifestyle away from us. I didn't know why, but it seemed all our problems were caused by my grandmothers. I was sure, though, that Gigi wasn't the source of my problems.

Then, without warning, Mother threw our things in a bag and jerked me out of the Palmer House dream world.

I found myself being dragged to a tiny, dirty apartment. On the back side of a several-story building, it had shadowy halls and equally shady residents.

Elevated train tracks ran outside the back wall, not far from the Bryn Mawr stop. Rear apartments at the same level as the "El" were the least desirable, and therefore the cheapest. The whole place shook when the trains roared and rattled by day and night.

Certain the ancient building would collapse, I slept poorly. Mother slept drunk.

The apartment had a small bathroom and living area. Built into one wall was a miniature kitchen nook with a refrigerator, sink, and stove. The bed where mother and I slept folded out of another wall. We had a table and couch, but no television or radio.

Mother's idea of mealtime made me wish I were back at the Home. The thrill of eating doughnuts for breakfast and sometimes lunch wore off quickly. Her meal preparation consisted of overcooking TV dinners in aluminum foil and slinging the blackened food on the table.

If I hesitated to eat, she yelled at me for criticizing her cooking and insisted it was fine. Hunger drove me to pick up my fork and find a way to chew and swallow burnt green beans, bone-dry mashed potatoes, and crunchy meatloaf—washing it all down with lukewarm tap water.

Mother often fell asleep in the middle of the day for hours, usually because she'd been drinking. When that happened, I didn't get any supper. I remember trying several times to jog her awake, but she wouldn't budge. Life was dark, noisy, irrational, and lonely. My entertainment consisted of comic books, imaginative games, and watching spiders and cockroaches crawl on the walls and floors.

It wasn't much fun when Mother was asleep; it was even less fun when she was awake. She spent most of that time lecturing. All I heard was her voice, no words. The talk suddenly would turn hateful and mean, punctuated by curses and pots and pans flying across the room. I was surprised that nothing she threw broke.

At the top of her hate list at the moment was the state of Illinois. She thought the government didn't give her enough aid or welfare money. One night, after a rant on that subject, I asked a question about money—and my father.

"When will Daddy be well enough to work and take care of us?"

Until now, no one really had explained why my father was "too sick to raise me." The most anyone had said was that he'd "hurt his brain" and was in a hospital too far away for me to visit.

My question seemed at first to stun my mother; she went limp as a flat tire. But then something inside seemed to fill her up, and the sadness on her face turned to rage.

Trembling with fury, she exploded. "Your father is a wimp and a loser! He left us and tried to kill himself by blowing his brains out with a gun. He must have changed his mind at the last minute, because he didn't even do that right. He's brain damaged, and will never get better."

Slowly the revelation sank in as she continued. "That's why he's never called or written us, Robby. That's why! He can't. The only way we'll ever be a family again is in heaven."

She poured herself another drink of cheap wine. I wondered whether she planned to kill us so we could all go to heaven and be together.

So that was what had happened to my father. *He shot himself in the head trying to kill himself?* And he would never get better. A familiar, heavy steel door seemed to clang shut on my hope for being a family again.

But living under Mother's "care" continued. I felt kidnapped, even if her legal custody of me would keep her from being charged with that crime. Abducting me seemed to represent a power game to her. "I guess I showed them," she spat as she burned my Children's Home clothes in a barrel in the alley. "You're my kid, and they'd better remember it!"

I wished she'd forget it. I wanted Gigi and Nola. I wondered why they wouldn't rescue me.

Later I learned that Gigi and the Home staff were in a panic. They had no idea where we were, or if I was safe or even alive.

Several weeks into my abduction, Mother called Gigi from a pay phone. My grandmother must have asked to speak with me; Mother held the phone so I could say a few words. Then she pulled the receiver away, shouted something about "showing you all," and hung up.

For nearly two months, Mother tortured my poor grandmother. If Gigi would be home at 8:00 on a particular night, Mother would say, I'd be allowed to call. Sometimes we would go to a pay phone and place the call, but if Mother was in a foul mood she skipped it. When we did call, she'd jerk the phone out of my hand after a minute or two and snap, "That's enough! Bye." When Gigi told me how worried everyone was, I didn't know what to say.

One night, with only a couple hours' notice, Mother agreed to let me have supper with Gigi. Mother wouldn't go up to the apartment with me or let me spend the night; she must have feared Gigi would take me back to the Home.

It was a feast: Boston pot roast, one of my favorites, with a mound of side dishes. There was enough for four, but my grandmother didn't touch a thing.

Even as I gobbled mouthfuls of food, I could tell Gigi was concerned about me. During one brief pause, I said, "Grandma, you really should eat some of this stuff. It's great!"

"I'm just not hungry, Robby," she said with a dejected sigh. I knew she was just making sure there was plenty for me.

It didn't occur to me to use the visit as a chance to escape from Mother. I'd resolved to accept life the way it was, no matter how rotten. I didn't realize that someone from the Children's Home might come and get me if I revealed where we were. Gigi didn't phone for help; maybe she was afraid of my mother.

Gigi did ask a lot of questions that night about where and how we were living, though. All I could tell her was that our ratty apartment was a couple of blocks from a movie theater on the lake side of the Bryn Mawr El stop.

That must have given her enough clues to lead the authorities to us. A couple of days later, a loud, insistent knock sounded on our apartment door. I didn't know what to do; it was the first time anyone had knocked.

"This is the police!" barked a voice that sounded like it belonged to a giant. "We have an arrest warrant. Open the door!"

I shook and shook my drunken mother to wake her. Finally she got off the couch, asked who it was, and opened the door. The policeman who put handcuffs on her looked enormous.

As we walked out of that terrible building, I thought at first that the policeman was arresting me, too. *What have I done now?* I wondered. *Where is he taking me? Maybe he's taking me back to the Home or to Gigi.*

I was shocked when the officer picked me off the ground and put me on a bench in the back of the "paddy wagon." There was a bench seat on each side, and a bar-covered window in the back. Not only could we look out, but motorists behind us could look in. I wanted to scream, "I'm not a criminal!" But it wouldn't have done any good. Once again, I was humiliated and powerless.

When Mother and I arrived at the precinct, we were separated. I didn't know where Mother was going, but figured I'd be taken to Gigi's apartment or back to the orphanage. But a policeman told me I'd be spending the night in the Audy Home.

Located near the Loop in downtown Chicago, the Audy Home was a holding area for children awaiting court decisions on their fates. It looked like a prison to me.

The man who checked me in sat at a desk. Behind him was a short hallway leading to four cells, two of which were occupied by screaming, swearing teenagers. They cursed the world and the man at the front desk, who occasionally cussed back.

His job was to list everything I had with me. "Watcha got on ya?" he growled.

"Shoes, socks, pants, underwear, a belt, shirt, and jacket."

Glaring at me, he said, "It's February in Chicago, kid. Ain't ya got a coat?"

"I'm wearing a coat," I replied, hugging my jacket closer.

"Well, which is it? A coat or a jacket?"

I didn't know. Searching his rock-hard face for a clue, I couldn't find one. My lower lip trembled as I blurted, "It's a coat!"

Jumping from his chair, the man swore at what he apparently thought was my sassy tone. He grabbed my arm and hauled me toward the cells. "Let me show you what happens to boys who don't respect me!" he yelled.

Picking me up, he pushed my face against the bars of a cell door. I saw a stained, dirty sink and a bucket that had been used as a toi-let. The smell was worse than the odor of manure that drifted over Princeton's farms in the spring.

"Do you want to spend the night in there?" the man bellowed.

"No, sir!"

Dragging me back to the front desk, he demanded, "Well, is it a coat or a jacket?"

"I don't know, sir," I squeaked. "I'm just a kid. I don't know!"

"It's a coat, stupid."

After ordering me to remove my clothes, he gave me something to wear that looked like a prison uniform. Then he told me to go upstairs to the unit where I'd spend the night.

When I reached the door at the top of the stairs, though, it was locked.

I knocked. No answer.

I knocked again. No answer.

I pounded until a kid finally started to talk trash through the door.

"Whaddaya want?" he yelled.

"I'm supposed to spend the night here."

"I don't know you."

"I want to talk to an adult."

"Why should I let you?"

"Open the door," I demanded.

"I don't have to open the door," he said with a sneer. "I don't answer to you."

"Just get an adult so I can get in there and not get in trouble."

"I don't care if you get in trouble. Why should I care about you?"

"Open the door or get an adult!" I said, trying to control my anger.

"Why should I let you in?"

"Because this is where I'm supposed to be!"

"Well, maybe I'll let you in," he said. "And maybe I won't."

Frustrated, I grabbed the knob hard. The door wouldn't budge. I was certain the mean guy downstairs would be up any minute to throw me into the filthy cell for failing to obey his order.

After a few more minutes of baiting, the kid on the other side of the door said he'd let me in after he got a look at me.

"Look through the keyhole so I can see ya."

I did. He spit—right through the keyhole. I caught it in the eye.

That was it! I yelled, screamed, kicked, and pounded on the door. The anger I felt when I got beaten by the older guys at the Home broke loose.

I was ready to take on the world. The next person who dared pick on me was going to get smashed to the ground, especially if it was the tormentor who'd spit in my eye.

A man finally opened the door and found a Tasmanian Devil staring at him. Without surprise or emotion, he calmly ordered, "Follow me. I'll show you where you'll sleep."

He brought me to a bedroom and told me to sit on one of its eight industrial-strength beds. "This is yours," he said. "I know you're angry, but I'm not here to deal with that. I'm here to manage the floor and keep you kids from hurting each other. Supper will be in less than half an hour. Please stay here until I come get you. I strongly suggest that you cool off."

His calm tone helped to defuse me before suppertime. Soon I was sitting in a cafeteria with bare, institutional-gray walls. A TV was perched behind wire mesh, too high to reach.

"Why only spoons?" I asked a fellow inmate.

"Don't be stupid," he snorted. "Forks and knives can be used for weapons!"

Later that evening, a guard told me to take a shower. One of the kids whispered, "Watch your backside."

The showers offered no privacy. Two teenage boys walked in with me. They must have read the fury on my face because they backed off and kept their distance.

Afraid somebody might jump me and beat me up, I sat up in bed until I was sure each of the other beds had a sleeping body in it.

Then I got up and walked to the barred window. Wrapping my arms across my chest, hands tucked into armpits, I hugged myself tight and rocked slightly from left to right as I'd done so many times before. Staring past the walls and their barbed wire, beyond the armed guards, I gazed at the sky and wondered why. Why this life? Why would no one rescue me? Was there a place for kids like me, and how could I ever get there?

This is a jail, I thought. *I'm eight years old and in jail. What did I do to get thrown into a place like this? What did I do?*

Some adult had told me I was only supposed to be here overnight, then back to the Home. I hoped things worked out that way. At least the Home didn't have bars on the windows, fences, guards, or my crazy mother.

I thought a lot about Mother that night. She treated people terribly. She blamed everyone else for her problems.

She didn't care about me. It was only a matter of time before she would blame her troubles on me. She was just like the older kids at the Home who lashed out at smaller ones for no reason, dumping their problems on someone else.

Under the spotlight of a guardhouse in a juvenile detention center, I made a vow: Never again would anyone make his or her problems mine. Not even Mother.

Finally, after double-checking that my enemies were asleep, I quietly slipped into bed and drifted off.

Next morning, after breakfast, a guard told me my caseworker had come to get me. I went to the courtroom, but didn't believe John was there until I saw his white shirt and dark hair. Going back to the Home wasn't going home, but it sure was better than the last couple of months.

As glad as I was to see John, he seemed even happier to see me. He tried to avoid getting overly emotional, but the softness in his eyes and voice told me how he felt.

As we walked out of that place, I wondered whether Nola's God felt the same way. Had her God seen me in the Audy Home or that rat-hole apartment? And if her God really cared, why was my life so miserable?

/6/

The Doctors

WHEN I RETURNED FROM MY months with Mother, I was hoping a few of the guys would be excited to see me. I wanted to hear, "Where've you been? What's been going on? Whadja do?"

It didn't happen. Instead I got a sad, "Hey, you're back."

In their eyes, my return marked failure. They didn't know if I was at fault, or if problems at home hadn't been fixed. They didn't even care. Whatever the reason, they figured my family had discarded me again.

Forget you, I thought bitterly. *When you want to know, I'm never going to tell you.*

Nola was concerned. She'd lost her puppy-dog kid. Now she was dealing with a wary mutt of a boy who'd been cold, hungry, and beaten down too many times. I was sullen and kept pretty much to myself.

I also drew some conclusions about castaway kids. Noticing that the Home had many more boys than girls, I decided that girls must be cuter and easier to raise than boys—so boys must be easier to throw away.

Nola kept trying, but failed to draw me back into the routine. I went through the motions, except when some other kid would push the wrong button and my rage would flash.

After a few weeks, John took me out of school one day.

"You've had a few rough months, Robby," he told me. "We're worried about you, so we're going to take the morning train so you can see some special doctors in Chicago who are going to make sure you're okay. We'll be there all day. I won't be with you, but I'll be in the building at all times, and we'll have lunch together. I promise. Then you'll meet with the doctors again, and we'll ride the evening train back together." He kept his word.

That night we rode the California Zephyr back to Princeton. After hours of testing and talking to doctors at a hospital, I was tired of sitting. John understood, so he let me take half an hour to explore the train and bought me a treat—a soft drink from the dining car.

Then he and I settled down in the nearly empty two-story observation car. I knew he wanted to talk. These caseworkers always wanted to "discuss" something.

As the train clickety-clacked down the rails, John asked about my day. I figured the faster I answered, the quicker I could get up again.

"Well, first, in the morning, they took me to a room with tables and toys. One of the docs gave me some small building blocks and told me to build a house, a barn, and a car. Then he gave me a pencil and asked me to draw a family and a home, and then color it in with crayons. I said okay, but asked why. The doc said he was going to measure my coggy skills, parts of logic, and flexes." I shrugged.

"Do you mean cognitive skills, spatial logic, and motor reflexes?" John asked with a smile.

"Yeah! That stuff! They didn't say draw a mom and dad, kids, and a house. They just said a family and a home. That was weird!"

John nodded, but didn't say anything.

"Then they told me to turn my back while they laid out a bunch of cards faceup. When the doc said 'Go,' I turned around and matched as many as I could until he said 'Stop.' "

John nodded.

"The first game I got 'em all and won!"

"Good for you, Robby!"

"Yeah, but the next couple of games were harder, and I didn't get them all done."

"That's okay, Robby. They didn't expect you to finish everything."

"How come they were writing things on a pad when we were having lunch?" I asked.

"They were making note of your table manners—how you handled a knife, fork, and spoon. How you acted in a casual setting with adults."

"Why?"

Using big words, John explained that sometimes after a childhood like mine and especially after being hidden for so long from everyone by my mother, many kids would be kind of messed up. They might get very angry at adults, or go backward and start acting like babies—or at least like younger kids.

John was quiet as I thought about what he'd just told me.

"I'm not going backwards," I decided out loud.

He nodded his head and smiled slightly.

I was glad he didn't ask whether I was angry. If he had, he would have gotten an earful.

"Did I do okay at lunch?" I asked.

"You did just great, Robby," he assured me. "Now, tell me about your afternoon with the psychiatrist."

I didn't want to; all I'd done all day was talk. Wouldn't he hear about it from the docs? Couldn't we just enjoy the train ride? But after years of monthly and now weekly caseworker meetings, I knew John would ask until I answered. So I slid down in my seat and went on.

"The psychiatrist was an okay guy, bigger than the other docs. He started off by telling me they couldn't help me if I wasn't honest. He wanted me to say what I was thinking, even if it hurt or sounded bad to be said out loud. He told me if they could understand how I felt about things, they could help me."

"What did you tell him, Robby?"

"I told him I'd try."

John seemed pleased, so I continued.

"The doctor wanted me to tell him about my father—what I remembered, what I knew, how I felt. That was hard. I don't remember him at all. I do have a photo of him. He had short, dark hair, and glasses. He had on a white shirt, a dark tie, a nice suit, and a big smile."

"What did you tell the doctor when he asked you how you felt about your father?" John asked.

"I don't know what I feel about my father because I don't remember him or know him. I told him I wish I had a real father who would play with me, carry me on his shoulders, and throw a football with me. I wish I had a father to be proud of, one who made me feel safe. And I'd maybe like to visit my father in the hospital, but maybe not. I think I understand why he was tired of living with my mother, but . . ."

I hesitated.

John waited for a long minute, then asked: "But what, Robby?"

I struggled. I'd never said this out loud to anyone.

"Please, Robby. You know I care. But what?"

Softly, almost in a whisper, I finally asked the question I dreaded hearing a "Yes" answer to. "But John, how could he leave me? Was he tired of me?"

John shook his head. Leaning forward, he looked deep into my eyes. "It wasn't about you, Robby. He didn't get tired of you, and you didn't do anything wrong. That's hard to understand at your age, but you must believe me. Your parents' choices have had nothing to do with you. Unfortunately, you've had to suffer from the things they've done."

I'd heard this from him many times before. I still couldn't find a way to believe it.

We sat in silence, watching the fields pass by. I hoped John was done with the questions, but I should have known better.

"So what else did the doctor ask, Robby?"

"He wanted me to tell him about my mother. I thought the whole world knew about her. She's crazy."

"Did the doctor ask you how you felt about that?"

"Yeah. I told him I had asked Gigi if my mother loved my father. Gigi said she supposed so, but she wasn't sure if Joyce really ever loved anybody but herself."

John waited again, then asked, "Is that how you feel about your mother, Robby?"

"Yeah. I don't know who she loves, but it's not me. And, well, this sounds bad, but I would like a break from seeing her until she can get some kind of better."

John nodded. "Don't worry, Robby. Your mother is in the Elgin State Mental Hospital and will probably be there for quite some time." He paused. "Anything else you want to talk about before we finish?"

"Can you tell me what they decided about me—the docs today? Am I going to be crazy, too?"

John thought for a moment, then said, "You're not crazy, Robby. You're a normal little boy. But you've been through a really tough time. We'll get their written report in a couple of weeks and we'll talk about it then. But they did say you're better than they expected you'd be. You've somehow been able to think through your emotions and that has helped you. It's quite amazing that you've been able to do that at your age."

And then came the words that registered in my heart: "They want us to get you into a normal home as soon as possible."

As the train clattered down the tracks, the phrase echoed in my head: *a normal home.*

It sounded good, and more than good. But after all that had happened, *was* it possible?

7

Gigi's Gift

A COUPLE OF MONTHS AFTER my visit with the Chicago doctors, Nola asked, "How would you like to spend the weekend with Gigi in Chicago, Robby? She wants to talk to you about something important."

"Wow! Can I really?"

"Sure. You'll go on Friday, have a nice visit, and next week we'll discuss what you two talk about."

Does this mean Gigi is going to take me? I couldn't wait to find out.

When Friday finally arrived, John dropped me off at my grandmother's apartment. The smell of baked chicken made my mouth water. I loved anything Gigi cooked, but her Boston pot roast, crunchy oven-baked chicken, stuffed pork chops, and chicken with rice and mushrooms were my favorites. "I love watching you eat, Robby," Gigi always told me. "It makes me happy."

It made *me* even happier. This time I ate twice as much as she did.

We always saved dessert until later. Usually after Gigi cleared the table we'd play dominoes or cards; she'd let me win, but never made it easy. Or I'd hide behind the curtain between the kitchen and living room and growl like a monster, then giggle when she screamed and pretended she was going to faint. We might have played tag or hide-and-seek, but the apartment was so stuffed with furniture there was hardly room to move.

On this night, though, Gigi looked serious. "Let's leave the dishes 'til later and sit on the couch. I want to talk to you."

I barely could stifle a grin. I just knew what she was going to tell me: I could come live with her.

She settled next to me on the couch. "Robby," she began, "I've tried to protect you. But now, after all you've just gone through, I think it's time to tell you a few things."

I twisted around on the sofa, trying to get comfortable. It seemed this was going to be a long story.

"Your Grandmother Pauline didn't like your mother," Gigi began. "She thought your father should have married a woman whose family was more like theirs socially and financially—in her words, 'more their kind.' "

Gigi's serious expression vanished, and she snickered. In a silly accent she said what I'd heard her say many times before: "But thee and me knows: Class ain't about cash, but character!"

If anybody had class, I thought, it was Gigi. I wanted to have it, too. If I lived with her, I would.

"When Pauline couldn't stop the wedding," Gigi went on, "she tried all she could to make the plans and direct the show." Mimicking Pauline with a syrupy Southern accent, she declared, "Now Joyce, dear, I only want the best for you and Robert."

It was my turn to snicker.

She shook her head, and her tone grew sarcastic. "Out of the obvious goodness of Pauline's heart, she went on to tell your father and mother what each and every detail of their wedding was to be. Your mother wasn't about to take that without a fight. It was as if the war between the North and South was still going on between those two headstrong females."

She rolled her eyes. "While your parents were on their honeymoon, your grandmother hired movers to take all the furniture out of their apartment and put it in storage. Then they brought in a bunch of expensive furniture Pauline had bought."

"Wow! Mother must have been really happy when she got back," I said.

"Happy? Oh, no, child! She and your father were furious that Pauline would buy such expensive furniture and move theirs out and hers in without discussing it with them or asking their permission. Your mother was like a hissing cat throwing fur, and your father was once again caught between his wife and his mother."

Pauline must be as crazy as my mother, I thought. *I wonder if our whole family is nuts.*

Gigi explained that after I was left at the Home, Mother began selling some of the furnishings at pawn shops. "I talked her into letting me keep some of the furniture and gifts here for safekeeping. I gave her my furniture for her apartment and $1,000 to pay bills with until she could find a job and get back on her feet."

"So that's why you have so much furniture in here?" I asked. "I wondered why your apartment was so full of stuff."

Gigi paused, took a deep breath, and the seriousness returned. She took my hand and looked deep into my eyes.

This is it, I thought. *She's going to tell me she can sell some of this stuff and keep me with her.* I sat up straighter and waited for the good news.

"Robby, I intend to live to see you graduate from college and get married."

What?

"All this beautiful mahogany furniture as well as the china, crystal, and silver is yours when I die, or sooner if you want it. I saved it for you! I'm glad I did because your mother would have sold it all and used up all the money. It's your inheritance. If you and your wife don't want it, then you can sell it and buy what you want. It will give you a good start on life."

Gigi was trembling. Thinking about me going to college, being a man, getting married—it made her feel mushy, I guessed.

But I was so disappointed I couldn't speak. I couldn't believe this was the big surprise.

Not knowing what else to do, I leaned forward and hugged my grandmother. She cried while I thought, *Shot down again.*

And this furniture stuff! Just one more weird story in my already weird life.

Eventually Gigi pulled back and wiped her tears. "Enough of this stuff," she announced. "Let's eat ice cream!"

So we did—vanilla with hot fudge and butterscotch.

As I lay in bed that night, my stomach was full. But I felt as empty as ever.

/8/

The Choice

NEXT MORNING, AFTER BREAKFAST, I still felt the disappointment as I watched Saturday morning cartoons on a small black-and-white TV behind Gigi's bedroom door.

She preferred radio. One of the shows she liked was a drama from Pacific Garden Mission. The stories were always about some down-and-out homeless person or drunk who hit rock bottom—then looked up, found God, and turned his life around. I wasn't into the God stuff, but Gigi was. When I listened, it was because of the hopeful message: No matter how bad life gets, it still can turn around and get better. I liked that idea, even though it didn't seem to apply to me.

Saturday was Gigi's day off from work, but we still took the El downtown to her place of employment—Marshall Field's. She wanted to show me off to her friends.

I could have spent the day watching the department store's huge train set, a network of vehicles, buildings, and mountains that had a man running it full-time. But Gigi's agenda was to let her friends tell me how big I was getting, to buy me a new shirt, and to go to the Walnut Room for dessert.

The Walnut Room was huge, paneled with rich walnut, with a ceiling that hovered many stories overhead. Small tables covered by white linen and napkins showcased the sparkle of crystal goblets and silverware. Waiters in white and black outfits reminded me of penguins.

The Frango chocolate with a hint of mint was wonderful. After stuffing myself as usual, I sat back and waited. Gigi seemed to be powering up for another talk. I hoped it would be better than the furniture story.

"Robby," she began, "as you know, your social worker and Nola and the doctors have been talking to me a lot about your future and what is best for you."

I sat up straight. The memory of an old hope peeked out from its hiding place.

Here it comes, I thought. *She's going to ask me to come live with her after all!*

"When your mother took you away for such a long time without permission, the Children's Home director went to the judge and had her removed as your legal guardian. Aunt Alice, your father's sister, is married to an attorney. He told me and your father's family that any one of us could become your legal guardian. So Arnold, one of your Grandfather Mitchell's brothers, has agreed to do that for you. You may not know this, but your father's father—Grandfather Mitchell—died three months after your father . . . after his accident."

What? What's she talking about?

I'm not staying with her? I'm going to go to some old guy I don't know?

And it wasn't an accident! He did it on purpose. Why won't adults talk straight to me?

Gigi must have read the confusion and anger on my face. "He's a nice man, Robby," she said quickly. "He lives in Atlanta, Georgia, and owns the Mitchell Motors Oldsmobile and Rolls-Royce dealership there. He has agreed to be your guardian. That way you will have someone from the family making decisions about what happens to you instead of the state or your mother."

"But, Gigi," I blurted. "Why can't I live with you?"

Her voice was surprisingly emotionless. "It's obvious there's no hope of your mother ever getting well enough to raise you. I pray every day that she gets well enough to get out of the sanitarium and move into a halfway house. Maybe then—just maybe—she'll be able to hold a job and support herself. But we don't think she'll ever be able to take care of you."

I nodded but didn't speak.

"Your father will never leave the Allen Mental Hospital in Georgia. He can walk but can't remember much, can't dress himself, and speaks so you can't understand him. He likes it when Uncle Arnold and your Aunt Alice come to see him, but gets angry when his own mother, your Grandmother Pauline, visits. In fact, he's gotten so bad I'm told she no longer visits him."

Why all this talk about my Georgia relatives? I don't even know them. They never cared about me before. Why now? What's Gigi trying to tell me?

"Robby, I love you with all my heart," she continued. "But I have to be practical. I'll be 70 next year, you know. That's too old to raise a spunky kid like you. You'll need a better place for a boy to grow up than with this old lady."

She winked, so I forced a chuckle to make her feel better. The tea room "penguin" refilled Gigi's cup as she opened her purse and took out an envelope.

"So, what are you going to do with me?" I asked.

"Let me read you part of a letter from the Chicago doctors. John gave it to me. 'How Robby escaped severe damage in the light of his background is a difficult question to answer. He sees himself as someone who has been cast aside. He wants to believe it's not his fault, but he must be moved from the institution before he loses his capacity to blossom into a socially and intellectually adjusted youngster.' "

More mumbo jumbo.

I repeated my question, but this time my tone was icy. "So what are you going to do with me?"

Gigi folded the letter and explained my three options. "You can stay at the Children's Home nine more years until you graduate from high school. You can visit foster families to see if you like one of them. Or maybe you can live with one of the Mitchell relatives in Atlanta."

She waited for my response.

No way I'm going to a foster home, I thought. My caseworkers had talked about that before, and I had said no.

Maybe there were good foster homes, I told myself, but how would I know? A kid who was matched with a good family never came back to the Home, so I never heard about it. The kids I knew only shared bad experiences.

They warned that if foster parents had children of their own, at least one of those kids resented the "intruder." Their advice: Don't go to a home with younger kids. Try one where you'll be the youngest.

Some of the boys I knew had lived in five foster homes before they were ten years old. Instead of feeling loved, they felt like stray puppies, trying to make their "keepers" happy. Caseworkers didn't seem to help when they warned that foster kids could be sent back to the Home if they didn't behave.

When I'd asked an older girl named Peggy what she thought, she'd said, "Don't go." She'd been reading a story about a young girl named Anne of Green Gables who was sent to a foster home. The people had wanted a boy to work the farm. When Anne arrived, the woman threatened to send her back. Anne had said something like, "I'll try to do and be anything you want, if you'll only keep me."

Peggy shook her head. "Well, you can bet I'm not going to do that, Robby. We're not circus monkeys to make some foster parents happy. I'd rather stay put at the Home than be thrown away again."

I understood.

Kids like us longed for a home with adults. We desperately wanted love, nurturing, security. But foster care put us with people who didn't necessarily have a long-term commitment to us. Key adults had already let us down; how could we expect anything better from strangers?

Reluctantly, I decided to try my Atlanta relatives. If that didn't work out, I'd just stay at the Home. It wasn't where I wanted to be. But after five years there, it was the only home I knew.

Gigi sipped her tea and waited.

"I want to live in a house with a family," I finally said. "I don't want to stay at the Home or go to a foster home either. I don't want to feel part of the foster family and then find out I'm being sent back to the Home for some reason."

Gigi seemed relieved. "I want you to do what you think is best for you, Robby," she said quietly. "But I have to admit I'm afraid foster parents might not let me see you. That would kill me."

"Can I try Atlanta, Gigi? Maybe when they get to know me they might take me. They're family, so I could still come and see you, couldn't I?"

Gigi hesitated. "I think so, Robby. But I might only see you once or twice a year." She took a deep breath and continued. "I understand why you don't want foster care, and that you don't want to stay at the Home until you graduate. I think it's a good idea for you to get to know your Atlanta family. I'll tell the Home it is okay with me."

She smiled and stood up. "Let's go watch the trains!"

I'd always enjoyed watching the conductor send toy trains round and round in circles. Somehow today it seemed fitting. I had no idea what track my life was on, and no way of knowing whether I would ever really get anywhere.

/9/

Atlanta

IT WAS TIME TO TALK with my caseworker about the future. But by now John had left the Home. I wasn't angry about his leaving. As far as I was concerned, he was just another adult who'd abandoned me, and I faced my next counseling session without enthusiasm.

The social worker, whose name and face I can't remember, was dressed in a stiffly starched white shirt and solid-color tie. Kids like us called guys like him "white shirts." Most of them seemed as stiff as their outfits.

"I'm disappointed you've decided against foster care, Robby," he told me. "I understand your feelings, but I think you're wrong. We've had many good placements, you know."

I listened, but my mind was made up.

"I guess we haven't done a very good job of showing you kids how good these homes are. You only see the kids who come back from the placements that didn't work out. We've got good homes with openings right now. We're not going to force you, but I still think you should give it at least one try."

"Thanks, but no thanks," I said, my voice soaked with sarcasm. "Not interested."

"Well, then, I'm glad you're willing to consider the family in Atlanta," he said with a smile.

"Why?" I asked, combative.

"It means you haven't closed the door on that option."

"I don't know why you and Gigi are happy about that. Those people don't want me. They're strangers. I've been here for five years and not one of them has ever come to see me."

"I know how that must make you feel," he replied. "But we really want you in a normal home. We don't want you here until you graduate."

I glared. "So now this place doesn't want me, either?"

Embarrassed, he stammered and sputtered. Before he could get his thoughts together, I burst out laughing.

I'd gotten him good with that one. Like many kids at the Home, I tried to control situations by throwing authority figures off balance. Some did it with bad behavior or explosive anger. I preferred twisting the grown-up's words and getting a reaction I liked.

When I finally stopped laughing and caught my breath, I said, "You should have seen the look on your face. It was *so* funny!"

He forced a half grin. *These caseworker types really need to learn how to loosen their ties and lighten up,* I thought.

"Okay, Robby, can we move on?"

Still snickering, I nodded.

"The fact that you're considering Atlanta is a good sign. It means you're still okay emotionally, so . . ."

I didn't hear the rest of what he said.

I'm not okay! I screamed silently. *There's no way that I'm okay.*

Didn't he realize that the only option I wanted was the one nobody talked about? Since age three I'd dreamed of the day Gigi would tell me I could live with her.

Her apartment is big enough for two, I thought. *For cryin' out loud, I know families of six that live in smaller apartments than Gigi's. I don't get it! It doesn't make sense that she won't take me. Mother's locked up and out of the way, so what's the hang-up here?*

I kept struggling to understand for the next few months, as the Home set up a summer visit with the Atlanta family.

Are they telling Gigi I'll be crazy like my mother? Does she think I'll be nuts like Pauline or my father? Or does she think I'm going to be a rotten teenager who'll only cause her trouble? I know she loves me, so what's the problem?

I didn't find an answer. Maybe it didn't matter. The adults had control; I couldn't change a thing.

So, like a drum with a steady but annoying beat, life at the Home went on as it had for six years—get up, get dressed, eat breakfast, go to school, suffer through the taunts, keep away from the bullies, come home, have a snack, run off some steam on the grounds, eat supper, do some homework, listen to the Bible story, get into bed, and think.

It took a lot of thinking before I seemed to hit on a solution. I decided the problem was money. Gigi didn't have enough to take care of both of us. Money was what we needed! I vowed to find a way to get some.

At the end of fourth grade, I flew with Gigi to Atlanta. It was exciting to be in an airplane; I didn't know any nine-year-olds in 1964 who'd flown in one.

The plan was for me to spend two weeks of summer vacation

with my relatives so we could get to know each other. After a few days, Gigi left. I was alone with Aunt Alice, my father's sister; her husband, Mack; and their three children, a girl and two boys. The oldest, Mack Jr., was only two months younger than I. Grandmother Pauline Mitchell lived with them, too.

If money was the problem, I'd come to the right place. These people had a bunch! Their three-story mansion in the Buckhead section of Atlanta, with huge rooms, tons of furniture, a library, chandeliers, five bedrooms, and three full bathrooms and two half-baths dazzled me. They had three tubs and five toilets for six people! It was a far cry from the Little Boys floor, where two tubs and two toilets had to suffice for sixteen of us.

Lucille, the full-time cook, lived there, too. She was quiet, with a medium build and black skin. We didn't have anyone with black skin in Princeton, a Swedish farming community. I'd seen some of what my mother called "those people" in Chicago, but didn't know any. Lucille, who'd worked for the Mitchells for over 40 years—since before Aunt Alice was born—seemed like part of the family. Even her apartment over the garage had a full bathroom.

They sure have enough room for me down here, I thought. *If we get along good, they won't have any reason not to ask me to live with them.*

My cousins and I claimed the magnolia-encircled yard as our outdoor play area, but it was second best to the family room in the basement. A full-sized pool table held the prime spot, accompanied by a Ping-Pong table, couches, fireplace, and bar.

Within days, my cousins nicknamed me "Frisky." My energy level was much higher than theirs. Soon they began to take turns playing with me, claiming I wore them out. "Hey, Sis, it's your turn," one of the boys would call as we finished an hour of pool, basketball, or street soccer.

When they tired of entertaining me at the house, they took me swimming at the Capital City Club's enormous pool. I'd never been to a country club before; all I knew was that this one looked really expensive.

Before my first visit to the Club, Uncle Mack took me aside. Tall and handsome, with full, dark hair and a pleasant but somehow distant smile, he looked down at me and said, "If you want anything to eat or drink while you're at the Club, Robby, just tell the waiter to put it on my bill."

Good deal! I thought. For the next two weeks I ate to my heart's content.

The Atlanta relatives seldom asked about my life at the Home. When they vaguely did, I hedged and changed the subject—afraid that if I told them too much, they'd think I was weird and wouldn't invite me back. I wanted them to think I was normal and ask me to stay.

For two weeks I pretended this was the life I was supposed to have. Everything was perfect—except Grandmother Mitchell.

She seldom left the upstairs bedroom. After sleeping until noon, she would buzz Lucille on the intercom and order breakfast. Sometimes she left by taxi to play bridge with friends or go downtown to the City Club. Most of the time she sat in her rocking chair and read or watched TV.

When her bedroom door was open, I was in trouble. Like a bird of prey, she seemed to listen for the sound of me running up the stairs. Then she would call out in a pitiful whine, "Robby, dearest, if you could please spare a minute for your old grandmother?"

Sometimes I'd tell her I had to hurry back downstairs because someone was waiting for me. But guilt usually had me reluctantly wandering into her room.

"Are you enjoying yourself?" she always asked. "Sit down and tell me all about what you've been doing."

After I mumbled a sentence or two, she'd take over. "I'm so happy you're living in such a wonderful place with so many wonderful little playmates and caring nannies," she often said.

I wanted to shoot back, "How do you know? You've never been to the Home and have never even asked me about it!" Instead, I kept quiet and hunkered down for what was sure to come next.

"Your mother—bless her heart—has nearly ruined you, Robby. But I'm going to help you now. It's important that you learn how to fit into proper society. Your general manners, especially your table manners, need quite the improving. For example . . ."

Then she'd lecture me about all the things I'd done wrong.

But she couldn't stay on the topics of gracious living and etiquette for long. Soon she'd begin on Mother. "Oh, Robby, I'm so sorry to speak ill of any person, but I know *that woman* has told you so many lies about me that I want you to know the truth. Joyce is a sick, confused woman. I'll never understand what your father saw in her."

Tears filled her eyes, but I wasn't moved. To me she was like an old prune, an actress saying well-rehearsed lines. She wore too much white, powdery makeup and too much lipstick. And why did an old woman have waist-length hair that was always in a bun on her head, like a little hat?

Pauline reminded me of the wolf in "Little Red Riding Hood," pretending to be a sweet grandmother but waiting for a chance to destroy. After bemoaning her son's poor choice of a wife, she'd shake her head and say, "I delicately tried to bring up things I noticed about her. But my dear, sweet Robert wouldn't listen to me. I can't understand why. After all, I wasn't being bossy or interfering; I just wanted the best for my precious boy."

When I couldn't stand any more, I'd interrupt her whining and ask, "May I be excused, Grandmother? When I came upstairs, I promised Mack I'd be right back so we could play."

She always let me go, but never without a sigh. I'd stand up, kiss her wrinkled, powdered forehead, and leave. I couldn't wait to get out of sight so I could wipe the taste of her off my lips.

Aunt Alice seemed to feel sorry for me when I got stuck in one of these sessions. She never asked about them, but if she had I'd have told her that nothing Pauline said made any impression on me. It seemed to me that the only difference between Pauline and my mother was that Pauline was rich and lived in a mansion instead of a mental hospital. Both were sick, filled with hate—hate for each other, for immigrants, for black-skinned people, and for any thing or person standing in their way.

Both ranted about Dr. Martin Luther King, Jr. and his marches for equal rights. After meeting the people who provided household help in Atlanta, I didn't understand such anger. They all had black skin, and they were all nice to me. Why would anyone hate them or think they shouldn't be treated the same as whites?

It was also clear to me that Pauline didn't love me any more than Mother did. I was just one more issue for them to fight over. If I hadn't been born, they'd be battling about something else. I wasn't the prize; power was.

I flew home from that visit by myself. "White Shirt" and Gigi met me at the airport in Chicago. All the way to Princeton I told them about the wonderful house, the great fun, how nice the family was, and how I couldn't wait to go back again. I didn't mention Pauline; her behavior didn't seem important enough to talk about.

As soon as we got back to the Home, Gigi kissed me good-bye and went to talk with my counselor before catching the train back to Chicago. I ran to tell Nola about my adventure.

"You won't believe it," I said. "The house is huge! The kids were great! We played pool and soccer and football and basketball and went swimming at the country club, and—"

The more I rambled, the bigger Nola's smile got. Finally it seemed to take over her face.

Is she laughing at me? I thought.

"Whatcha smilin' about?" I asked.

"This reminds me of *Oliver Twist.*"

"Who's Oliver Twist?" I asked. "Did he come to the Home while I was gone?"

Nola chuckled. "*Oliver Twist* is a story about a boy separated from his family, put in an orphanage, then rescued when it turns out his family is very wealthy."

I got excited. "Can I meet this kid?"

"Oh, no, Robby. Oliver is a boy in a storybook. You'll read about him in high school."

I frowned in confusion.

"It's not a true story, Robby. It's an old, very famous story, written by a man named Charles Dickens."

"Do you think I'll be like the kid in the story?"

"Well, as much as you like to eat and as determined as you can be, I sure can see you walking up with your bowl, asking, 'More porridge, please?' "

Her chuckles turned to laughter. I didn't have a clue what she was laughing about, but it was so contagious that soon I was giggling, too.

Finally she caught her breath. "Oh, Robby, that's just a famous scene in the book. I'm sorry. I just couldn't help but imagine you in that scene."

I still didn't get it, but all that mattered was that she wasn't laughing at me. "So you think I might be like Oliver Twist and get rescued by my own rich family just like he did?"

As she had so many times before, Nola knelt. She pulled me to her for a hug.

"I hope so, Robby. I really, really hope so," she whispered.

It sounded like more than a hope. It sounded like a prayer.

/10/

Is There Room?

IF FAITH IS THE ASSURANCE of things hoped for, I had faith for the first time in years that my life might finally become normal. Living with my rich relatives became my dream. I had to make a great impression on them during my next trip.

Fifth grade dragged by. Finally summer vacation arrived, and I was on a plane back to Atlanta.

Aunt Alice and cousin Mack picked me up at the airport. When we got to their home in Buckhead, I hauled my suitcase up to my bedroom.

That's when Uncle Mack called me into his room and shut the door. "Sit down, Robby. I've got to tell you something."

My heart began to race. *He's the man of the house!* I thought. *He's gonna tell me I get to stay.* I trembled with excitement.

"Last summer," he began, "when I told you to order what you wanted at the Club, I didn't mean you could order everything on the menu!"

I could feel my face turning red as a beet. Uncle Mack chuckled.

"Robby, I'm not trying to make you feel bad. Just follow the example of my children and eat less, please."

I was crushed. Stammering, I barely managed an apology.

All year I'd planned to be so wonderful that this family would beg me to live with them. Now, within the first hour, it looked like I'd blown my chance!

How could I have been so stupid the first time I was here? I asked myself. Worse, I didn't know how much it was safe to eat now.

So I looked to cousin Mack for direction. At the Club I ate only what he did—sometimes less.

When the shock of that first conversation wore off, things seemed to look up. My cousins laughed a lot; so did Uncle Mack. I figured he'd forgiven me, and that they all still liked me. My hope grew stronger when Aunt Alice made sure I spent time with Grandfather Mitchell's brothers and their families. I liked them, and especially hit it off with Uncle Arnold and his wife, Annis.

Arnold was tall and lean with a Roman nose, big smile, and hearty laugh. Owner of the Rolls-Royce and Oldsmobile dealership, he had a great home on three acres in downtown Atlanta and a 150-acre farm in the country. Near the end of my second week, I spent a couple of days at the farm working, fishing, and playing.

Aunt Annis was tall, a self-described "country girl" with salt-and-pepper hair. At each meal she would ask me, "How can you inhale so much food, child?" I couldn't seem to help myself; the Home didn't serve fried fish or fried chicken with homemade biscuits dripping with butter and honey. The variety of vegetables—squash, tomatoes, okra, greens, black-eyed peas—went far beyond the potatoes, corn, and "government" canned green beans I was used to. The Home had no ice cream, either—and here it was unlimited!

My time there whizzed by. As I said good-bye to Uncle Arnold, I worked up the courage to ask the question that was uppermost on my mind.

“Can I come back and live here, maybe?”

His smile was warm and polite. “Maybe, Robby,” he said, ruffling my hair. “Grab your bag; it’s time to get going. Aunt Alice and Uncle Mack are waiting to drive you to the airport.”

At the gate before I boarded the plane, I tried again. With a big grin and my fingers crossed, I said, “Thank you for the visit. I love being here. Do you think maybe I can come back and live with you guys?”

Uncle Mack’s response was to shake my hand as if I were a client in his law office. Aunt Alice hugged me lightly.

Neither one answered.

Still, when I got back to the Home, I didn’t give up. I began to ask Nola regularly whether my uncles had called about my going to live with them. No one had.

When I saw Gigi each Saturday for the rest of the summer, I asked whether she’d heard from Atlanta. Each week she answered, “Be patient, Robby. I’ll talk to them. I promise.”

By late August I couldn’t stand it any longer. “Gigi,” I asked, exasperated, “what about me going to live in Atlanta? Haven’t you talked to them?”

“We’ve talked, Robby. But there’s no news yet.”

She tried to change the subject, but I wasn’t about to let her.

“Tell me what they said, Gigi. I know they liked me. They’ll take me, Gigi. I know they will. I made them laugh!”

She patted me on the head. “Perhaps this isn’t a good time for them,” she said. “Maybe things can be worked out later.”

Later?

I didn't want later. I wanted now.

It wasn't clear whether there was a place for me in Atlanta. Soon I learned there was no place for me in Little Boys.

The week before school started that fall, Nola dropped a bomb. "It's gotten crowded on Little Boys, Robby. We need to make room. Since you're going into sixth grade, and we think you're ready, we're going to move you up into Big Boys."

"Nola," I protested, "I'm not a big boy! I'm only just going on 11. I'm not even 5 feet tall. I don't weigh a hundred pounds. Some of those guys are giants! They're old, Nola—16, 17, 18!"

"I'm sorry Robby, but it's the only thing we can do. We have too many little boys right now, so something has to change. We're not trying to be mean; it's just what has to be."

"But . . . I'm gonna get hurt up there!"

"I'm sorry, Robby, I'm truly sorry," she whispered. Then, like a mama bear who knows it's time to leave her cub behind to fend for itself, she turned and walked away.

The Big Boys houseparent helped me to move to the new building and showed me to my room. As I carried my box of belongings down the hall, one of the big boys yelled, "Fresh meat on the floor!" Muffled laughter followed.

My new roommate wasn't there when I arrived. Nola had told me he was three years older than I, but assured me he was nicer than most of the other guys.

He turned out to be okay. But he didn't stand up for me or become my friend. I was alone in a den of lions.

I soon learned that those lions had a plan for me. Every day, one way or another, I was going to get smacked. Every day some older boy was going to remind me I was on the bottom of the pecking order. It wasn't a question of whether the punishment would be administered—only who would do it.

I wasn't the only victim. Typically, an older boy would come home in a bad mood and take it out on the nearest kid. A black eye or visible blood meant getting in trouble, so these guys never left obvious marks. A knuckle to the head was one of their favorites; it left painful bumps hidden by hair. Forearm smashes delivered in the hall were popular, too.

If I came out of my bedroom and saw one of the "mean guys" coming down the hall, I'd step back into my room and shut the door. Unfortunately, our doors had no locks. Sometimes the guy went right by, but more often than not he'd barge into the room after me.

One of the really big, really mean guys never went by. He always burst in, slammed me back, and sandwiched me between the door and the wall. Sometimes that was enough to satisfy him. Otherwise he'd pick me up, my legs and arms flailing, and fling me across the room. One well-placed blow to my head, and he was on his way without leaving a trace.

I was no match for these bullies, but couldn't seem to stop myself from fighting back. When I complained to Nola on the playground, she replied, "I've never seen you start a fight, Robby. But I've never seen you walk away from one, either. You might try that sometime. You'll find it will take all the fun out of this game the big guys are playing."

She was probably right. But even if I'd had the self-control to walk away, I didn't want to. I wanted to smash my enemies until my anger and frustration were gone.

They never left, though. They only grew worse.

Soon my efforts to vent that rage took a dark turn. I couldn't defeat my human tormentors, so I began taking my frustrations out on defenseless animals.

It started when I asked Gigi to give me a chemistry set for Christmas that year. She complied, thinking I wanted to become a doctor or scientist. On Saturday afternoons I would grab a few bottles of chemicals, hop on my bike, and ride several miles to the creek that ran by the town dump.

No one bothered me there. But plenty of frogs were on hand for my experiments.

At first I investigated which of the chemicals blinded them. For a while I got a cruel satisfaction from watching them hop around, banging into things, but I tired quickly of that game.

I turned to blowing things up. In science class we'd learned that certain chemicals mixed together created explosions. Stolen fertilizer and firecrackers became my weapons of choice, and the frogs my victims. I named them for the bullies on my dorm floor, then blew them up.

Watching the stand-ins for my tormentors explode seemed to make me feel better, at least temporarily. But it didn't solve my problems. I made it through sixth grade without being discovered—and without getting any closer to a real home than I'd ever been.

That summer, I flew to Atlanta again. Once again I felt like an actor in a tragic comedy—warm welcome, lots of fun, trying hard, asking whether I could live with them before I started seventh grade.

And once again, the same silence.

It was time for junior high. I looked forward to a new start in a new school.

Gigi bought me two pairs of pants and two shirts. I was so proud of them; each day during the first week I switched them around to make different combinations.

Not everyone was impressed. At the end of that week, a girl in my homeroom looked me up and down with disgust. "Not *that* shirt again," she hissed. "Are those the only clothes you have?"

I was too stunned to answer. But moments later I was screaming silently at her.

These are the best clothes I have! They're new, not hand-me-downs. Too bad my wardrobe doesn't suit you, your Highness. I can't help it. This is all Gigi could afford.

I wanted to smash that girl in her snooty face and make her eat my lousy shirt. Once again, I was on the outside looking in.

Seventh grade would be no better than any other. The location was new, but the struggle wasn't. I spent the year at the fringe of the cliques, and continued to serve as a punching bag for the bigger guys at the Home.

A different child boarded the plane for Atlanta the following summer. A volcano boiled inside me.

I've gotta get out of the Home before I do something stupid, I thought. *This may be my last chance. I have to find out what Uncle*

Mack and Aunt Alice want me to be so I can stay with them. I've just got *to.*

Soon after I got to Atlanta, though, my plan screeched to a halt.

"Uncle Warren is taking you to Greensboro, North Carolina, next week," Aunt Alice told me. "That's where he and your Grandfather Mitchell and all their brothers and sisters grew up. The North Carolina family is gathering for a picnic, and you're invited."

She spoke as if this were a great treat. I had my doubts. I'd spent only a few hours with this uncle, an insurance salesman and the oldest of the brothers. What could we possibly talk about on such a long trip?

Then I realized Uncle Warren could be part of my plan. *Hey, dummy,* I told myself, *this will be a good time for you to dazzle this guy. Then he'll be on your side when you ask to stay.*

For the next week I worked doubly hard to be polite and helpful to Aunt Alice, Uncle Mack, and the cousins. I didn't ask the waiter at the City Club to put anything on the tab. I even spent time with Grandmother Pauline.

When it was time to go to Uncle Warren's house, I said goodbye to my cousins. Then I turned and hugged Aunt Alice.

"Maybe I can come back and live here," I said. "I'll ask Gigi if that's okay with her."

I watched closely for a response. Her warm smile turned into a blank mask.

She didn't say, "That will be great!"

She didn't say, "We'll think about it."

She didn't even say, "I'm sorry, Robby, that probably won't work out."

She didn't say anything at all.

I told myself it was because she had three kids already. I told myself she probably thought I'd be one more than they could handle.

By now I knew what a closed door looked like. This door was closed. It was time to try knocking on another.

I'll have to be especially nice to Uncle Arnold and Uncle Warren, I thought. *One of them will surely take me in.*

I spent a few days on the farm with Aunt Annis and Uncle Arnold before he dropped me off at Uncle Warren's house. As we said good-bye, I gave it one last try.

"Uncle Arnold, I really love being with you," I told him. "Do you think maybe you and Gigi can work it out so I can come back and live with you?"

He nodded, but only in polite understanding. There were no words of hope.

As always, the loud silence said everything I didn't want to hear.

11

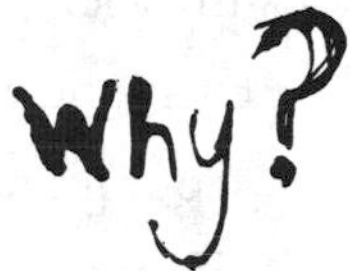

UNCLE WARREN'S CADILLAC SEEMED AS big as a boat. As we drove along, he told endless stories about my father's family.

I learned that my grandfather, Bob Mitchell, was the third oldest of eleven children. Uncle Warren was a year older. All the Mitchell brothers had large, Roman noses. Five of the brothers were tall; four were short and squat. Uncle Warren was one of the short and squat.

The nine boys and two girls were supported by their father, a dirt-poor tenant farmer. In 1910 he hauled bricks in his mule-drawn wagon to help build Guilford College in Greensboro, North Carolina.

Many years later, my Grandfather Mitchell and some of his brothers somehow managed to go to school there. After establishing their careers, they bought a house for their parents in Greensboro and kept them financially comfortable in their old age. One of Grandfather Mitchell's sisters and her husband lived there, too, taking care of her parents until they died.

With that illustrious history, the extended North Carolina family was gathering again for its annual picnic.

When we drove up to the house, I couldn't believe how many people were there. There must have been 50 adults and a bunch of kids my age.

Everyone welcomed me warmly. It was a huggy, friendly family.

"Your grandfather was a saint growing up," one aunt told me.

"He was a saint all his life," another added. "Can you imagine living with Pauline?" The uncles laughed.

I know what you mean, I thought.

Despite the welcome, though, I felt only a numb confusion. *How come Gigi didn't tell me about these guys? Uncle Mack and Mack Jr. don't talk about them. Grandmother Pauline didn't mention them either.*

Not one of these North Carolina relatives has ever tried to contact me. Did they even know I was alive?

Soon I was playing ball with some of the boys my age, but still felt like an outsider. When the adults asked about my interests in school and sports, they didn't mention the Children's Home. It was as if everyone had been warned to leave that topic alone.

That night, as I drifted off to sleep, my thoughts whirled. *Okay, they know I'm in an orphanage. They must know I don't want to stay there. So why don't they invite me to live with them?*

Have they heard stories from Pauline that I'm a bad kid? Do they hate my mother? What's going on?

The Atlanta uncles sure aren't going to ask me, so why not one of these guys? I'm no older than some of their kids. I could fit right in.

The next day Uncle Warren took me to see Guilford College. I was about to ask the questions I'd been thinking about last night when he made a stunning announcement.

"You know, Robby," he said, "if you keep your grades up, you'll be able to go to Guilford. After our parents died, we Mitchell boys funded a scholarship to the college in their honor. You're covered by it if you have the grades to be accepted."

I couldn't believe it. *I can go to college? Nobody from the Home gets to go to college!*

As far as I knew, only one guy had ever done that. He'd gone on a basketball scholarship after being at the Home for only a year and a half.

Most of the guys left the Home when they were 18, some without bothering to graduate. Those who finished high school didn't get to go to college. I knew several who'd ended up dead or in prison before they reached 21. The rest seemed to disappear, often working in dead-end jobs.

I remembered mentioning college in a "bull session" with other boys at the Home. The older guys had howled with laughter. "Yeah, right," one said. "Even if we were smart enough, which we ain't, where would we get the cash?"

"Quit your dreamin', kid," another chimed in. "You're gonna be stuck right here until they throw you out. Then you'll bum around like the rest of us. There's no college in your future, boy. Not a chance! Colleges only take good kids, and kids like us aren't good enough."

I'd thought of saying something like, "Maybe I'll be lucky," but had kept my mouth shut. *He's right,* I thought. *I'm not smart, and Gigi doesn't have enough money to send me. The dentist said I needed braces, and White Shirt told him there wasn't enough money for that kind of stuff. If there's no money for braces, there sure isn't any for college.*

And if college was only for good kids, that left me out, didn't it?

I'd been abandoned in an orphanage. Surely that proved even Nola's God thought I wasn't a good kid.

That memory came back vividly as Uncle Warren and I strolled across the Guilford campus. I couldn't believe it was happening.

Even the college president seemed happy to meet me. "Guilford College is proud to have graduated so many Mitchell men," he said. "We really appreciate your family's generosity. You have a place at Guilford, too, young man. Study hard, so when you graduate from high school you can take advantage of the scholarship waiting for you."

But by the time the tour was over, the importance of the scholarship began to shrink. The questions of the night before came rushing back, along with the anger I felt over the family that seemed to have rejected me.

The drive back to Atlanta and the flight to Chicago were spent trying to stifle the rage inside me that wanted to explode.

Back at the Home, I demanded a session with my new counselor, a guy named Marv.

"What the horse manure is going on?" I shouted as I stormed into his office. I slammed the door, then paced back and forth in front of his desk.

Marv was shocked. He'd seen me frustrated and cold and distant. But he'd never seen me in this kind of fury.

"I've had it with this God-forsaken life I'm living!" I yelled, banging my fist on his desk. "Who's doing this to me? Huh? Tell me! Who am I supposed to be mad at?"

"Calm down, Robby," Marv said softly. "Why don't you sit down, and we'll talk."

"I'm tired of talking! I don't want to sit down. I want someone to give me a straight answer."

"What's the question?"

"Are you stupid? I want to know who's doing this to me. I want to know who to hate!"

"Doing what to you, Robby?"

"Shutting me out of Atlanta or North Carolina, you pighead. Tell me! Who? I've been in this stupid Home since I was three. That's going on nine years! I have a family in Atlanta and more of them in Greensboro. My *own father's family*, for cryin' out loud! And they're not just comfortable. They're not just middle-class. They're filthy rich!

"There are over 40 families in that area that could raise me, Marv. And when I asked some of them to take me, I got silence! Do you hear me? *Silence!* No one even had the guts to tell me to my face, 'It ain't gonna happen, Robby. You ain't living with us.' "

My voice rose as the fury continued to build. "Why, Marv? I'm not that terrible a kid! I didn't ask to be born. I didn't ask for my alcoholic father to abandon me. I sure didn't ask for my psychotic mother! Are they punishing me because of them? Why won't anybody take me? *Why can't I belong to someone and have my own home?*"

From deep inside, the rage burst into a scream. My fist went forward, and before I knew it I'd punched right through the wall.

Marv jumped. Heavy footsteps came running down the hall. The door flew open. Another male caseworker stepped in.

"You okay in here, Marv?"

"Yup."

The man glared at me, but I glared back. "Don't worry," I said. "I'm not going to kill *him*."

The caseworker looked at Marv, who nodded. Finally the guy left the room.

"Close the door behind you!" I yelled.

"Sit down, Robby," Marv said. "Please."

My anger spent, I slumped into the chair and stared at the floor.

Marv kept silent for several minutes, thinking. I couldn't help but notice that he looked kind of like Abraham Lincoln—tall, slender, with a trimmed beard.

At length he spoke up. "We've struggled with that same question, Robby. I'm going to be honest with you, but you're not going to like my answer."

Glaring, I waited.

"I'll keep all the psycho-mumbo-jumbo out of it and say it plain," Marv began. "The only answer is that Gigi isn't willing to let go of you. She won't be able to see you as much if you go to Atlanta." He stopped and waited for the explosion.

I stared at the floor. Having already thought long and hard about this, I just needed a minute to get my ideas organized. At last I calmly looked up and said, "I understand what you're saying, Marv, but you're wrong. I see how you could think that, but I've already asked Gigi about it."

"Really? When?" a surprised Marv blurted.

"I asked her when I flew back from Atlanta this summer."

"What did you ask her?"

"I told her my father's relatives in Atlanta and North Carolina had the family and money to raise me, yet it was clear they wouldn't. I told her Aunt Alice and Uncle Mack liked me. Uncle Arnold and Aunt Annis liked me, too. Yet they weren't going to take me. Uncle

Warren was okay, but I didn't think any of the family in North Carolina were interested in me at all. She didn't say anything, so I held her hand, looked her straight in the eyes, and asked, 'Am I stuck here because you don't want me to go so far away?' "

"What did she say?"

I took a deep breath before going on. It felt good to be in control of the conversation for a change.

"She started to cry. She held me and cried hard for a long time. Finally she wiped her face and shook her head and said, 'It's not that, Robby. Your whole childhood has broken my heart. There's nothing I wouldn't do to try and give you a normal life. Even if that means I can only see you once a year.' "

I paused, then continued without much emotion. "I believe her, Marv. Gigi never lies to me. She hasn't always told me everything, but she has never lied to me."

I glanced up. Marv nodded, so I went on.

"Gigi told me she was sorry Atlanta wasn't going to work out. She was sure it wasn't me. She wouldn't explain why it wasn't going to work out, though. I'm not sure if she knows and isn't going to tell me. Or she knows, but really doesn't know how to explain it. Whatever the reason, I don't believe it's Gigi. So, if it's not Gigi, Marv, then who is it, and why?"

We sat in silence for a long time.

Finally Marv spoke up. "I truly have no idea, Robby. I'm being totally honest with you, too. I thought it was Gigi, but now I don't. I'm leaning towards your point of view, but that leaves me with no answer for you.

"If Atlanta is truly closed, and you're not open to a foster home, then we have to find a way to help you get through the next five years until you're old enough to be on your own. Are you ready to help us deal with your anger?"

I stood up. "I'm not angry with you, Marv. Or with Gigi." I walked to the door, opened it, and looked back. "And I'm not ready for you to help me deal with my anger, either. The truth is, I don't want to deal with it. I just want to hurt somebody."

My voice was like ice, but the fire of my rage burned hotter than ever.

/12/

Earning Power

I'VE GOTTA MAKE SOME MONEY!

If my future was in my own hands, if relatives weren't going to take me in, if Gigi couldn't afford me, it was time to look for a job.

I was only 12 that August of 1967, but ready to see if I could make money and have some "stuff." It was time for me to grow up and prove to Gigi I could be a man.

When kids like us made it through high school and graduated, we had to leave the Children's Home by August. Each boy was sent on his way with a new sports coat, a one-way bus ticket to the destination of his choice, a handshake, and a "Good luck, kid." We entered the adult world without the security of money, family support, or a good reputation.

After my visit to Guilford College, I realized my future was up to me. If I studied hard, worked hard, and saved money, maybe I had a shot at a better life. Maybe I could even get to be like my Atlanta family, at ease in a world filled with money and power.

Grandfather Mitchell had been well-to-do, and six of his brothers were millionaires—a rare thing in the 1960s. I hoped their good fortune would rub off on me.

Before his death, Grandfather had been a top-notch salesman for an industrial supply company that made leather belts that turned millions of machines during World Wars I and II. Some of his brothers, technically my great-uncles, were millionaires already. Uncle Bill made his fortune selling office supplies and equipment in Washington, D.C. Uncle Arnold had been an attorney, then gave up his law practice to sell cars. Tom owned Jeep and Buick dealerships in Atlanta; Howard sold Cadillacs in Florida; Warren made his fortune in insurance. After each summer's visit, I wondered how I could be rich, too.

So, on a hot summer Saturday before I entered eighth grade, I walked all over Princeton looking for a job. I didn't think anyone would give me one, but I aimed to try.

Every business I stopped at gave me a quick, "No!" I wasn't sure if it was because I was 12, or because they didn't trust kids from the Home.

At the end of a long, miserable afternoon, I ended up at the lumberyard by the railroad tracks. The owner was leaning against a stack of boards. Squaring my shoulders and standing tall, I walked up to him and announced, "I want a job, sir. I don't care what it is. Would you please give me a chance to work for you to prove I will work hard? Please, sir, just give me a chance."

Eyes set deep in a weathered face looked me up and down. The man bit his lower lip and stared. I looked back with confidence, knowing that two years of weightlifting had made me look more like fourteen than twelve.

Maybe it was my self-assurance. Maybe it was seeing a kid still wet behind the ears having the gumption to ask for work. Whatever the reason, he finally said, "Okay, boy. Come back next Saturday. I'll give you something really tough to do. If you do it, you've got the job."

When Saturday came, I couldn't wait to get there.

"You ready to work, boy?" the owner asked.

"Yes, sir," I replied.

A boxcar had just arrived. It was full of 50-pound bags of concrete powder, stacked on pallets. Employees were using a forklift to move the pallets off the train and set them outside a storage building.

"I want you to unload each pallet. Carry each bag into the storage shed and stack it up neatly," the owner instructed. Then, with a wink at the two men standing there, he walked away, whistling.

When I finished, I'd moved about two and a half tons of concrete. Sweat dripped from every pore of my body. Even the muscles that controlled my ears screamed with pain.

But I pulled myself up tall and walked over to the owner. Surprisingly, he didn't call an ambulance when he got a close look at me.

"I did it, sir," I said in a trembling voice. "Do I have the job?"

"Son, you have more than earned the right to work here." His smile was so wide it erased half his wrinkles. "Be back here next Saturday around seven."

The orphanage was only five blocks from the lumberyard, but I wasn't sure my quivering legs could stagger that far. Gathering every ounce of grit I had left, I stuffed my $2 pay into my back pocket and walked tall until I got out of sight. Then I slumped my shoulders, let my arms hang, and inched my way back to the Home.

Climbing the stairs to the second floor seemed impossible, but I did it. When I collapsed onto my bed, I nearly wept from the pain.

I worked at the lumberyard every Saturday for the next two years—for about 25 cents an hour. I mowed lawns, too, using the Home's riding mower and paying for the gas. For two summers I clipped corn tassels and bagged them for feed companies, which used them to germinate new seeds. It was hard, hot, itchy work.

Baling hay didn't pan out, due to allergy-induced sneezing fits that nearly killed me. But I toiled at a car wash and shoveled snow from driveways. Sometimes I headed to class in work clothes with snow in my hair and sweat frozen in my eyebrows. The schedule was tough, but I managed to earn money and still be involved in sports.

Around that time I read *Up from Slavery* by Booker T. Washington, the slave turned educator. Instantly he became one of my heroes. Labor was no disgrace, he wrote; he learned to love it, not just for the money but for the sake of the work itself. He found that doing something the world wants brings independence and self-reliance. I was beginning to understand what he was talking about.

He was also into that Bible stuff. It was there that we parted company.

That year I suffered through confirmation classes at a local church. Some of it was interesting. But when the class was over, I created an uproar by saying I didn't want to join the church.

Nola was drafted to talk me into joining. Her approach was gentle, but I still wasn't buying.

"I can't relate to the Jesus they taught about," I told Nola. "Besides, if God is so good, why am I here?"

Nola knew when to back off, and did just that. The leaders of the church and Home made it obvious they weren't happy. I was the only kid who refused to join.

I didn't care. I was making money, and money was going to save me.

Knowing I couldn't leave cash in my room at Big Boys, I opened a savings account at the bank. Some of that came from family gifts—like the $10 and $20 bills Uncle Arnold occasionally sent, and the $100 he gave me one Christmas. Uncle Tom and Uncle Warren had found out about their brother's generosity and matched it, allowing me to go home one summer with the staggering sum of $200.

My savings account was a closely guarded secret. Some of the guys already resented me for having a loving grandmother, better clothes, and a vacation in Atlanta every year. It didn't make sense to rub it in.

I tried to save at least half of my gifts and earnings. As my account slowly grew, so did my confidence. Independence was my goal, and it seemed money was the way to get there.

I'm gonna survive when I get out of this place, I vowed. *I won't end up homeless like Mother or rot in prison like some of the punks before me.*

Having money to spend wasn't my only goal. Accumulating it was also a game. Just as my uncles used money to keep score in life, I wanted to see how much I could bank before graduation. I hoped to have enough to keep me afloat until I could find a real job.

When I had the urge to splurge, I reminded myself that I'd need the money to stay out of jail. We rarely heard about guys from the Home who did well; we just heard the bad stories, and there were many.

My plan was to have $3,000 in the bank by the time I graduated from high school. *That will get me a couple of years in an Illinois state college*, I told myself, *or a brand-new Ford Mustang. The Guilford deal might fall through, and I'm not sure I want to go to North Carolina and be so far away from Gigi.*

My great-uncles always talked about investing in stocks. Eventually, as soon as I'd saved enough money, I did just that—buying shares of two Illinois firms whose products I enjoyed, McDonald's and Playboy.

Financially and otherwise, my goals in life were beginning to change. Instead of working for "stuff," I wanted money so I could dress well. Instead of settling for passing grades, I wanted good marks so I could get into college. Instead of floating toward a life of emptiness, I wanted to become a man with a future.

Determined not to be a punk like some of the guys at the Home, I vowed that nobody was going to visit me in prison or cry at my funeral when I was 21.

Still, I had no idea how to make that happen.

/13/

Reunion

WHEN I WAS IN EIGHTH grade, they let Mother loose.

At the time—1967—it was widely believed that people in institutions could live on their own or in group homes. Mental health advocates petitioned for the release of patients. Elgin State Mental Hospital, like numerous other facilities, released many—including Mother.

We hadn't seen each other for a couple of years. I didn't miss her at all.

Since I felt a little guilty about that, my counselor Marv thought it would help if I went to see her. He made arrangements for Gigi to take me there.

When the day arrived, I boarded the train to Chicago. The next day Gigi and I went downtown. We met Mother in a run-down restaurant near the halfway house where she lived.

Gigi had tried to prepare me for what I'd see. "You'll be surprised at your mother's appearance," she'd warned.

Surprised didn't come close. I was stunned when I saw how bad Mother looked.

She'd always been slim. But on this day her sunken cheeks made her look like people I'd seen in prisoner-of-war photos. Her hair was the color of dirty snow. If she'd tried to comb it, it hadn't worked; clumps stuck out all over the place.

Her faded, light-blue castaway dress, a relic of the 1950s, had short sleeves with white cuffs, a row of buttons down the middle, and a white plastic belt. The flared skirt was paired with ankle socks and sneakers. The outfit, dotted with stains and cigarette ashes, looked like a wrinkled sack.

That was bad enough. But what really got to me, and made my stomach tighten into a sick knot, was the look in her eyes.

I knew the look of people who'd lost hope. A glimmer was gone. I'd seen that empty look often in kids who came and went through the Home. Nola once called it "the long-lost look" that kids like us had as we stared into eternity, wondering why no one was going to rescue us.

Two brothers at the Home had the look. Their parents and two sisters had disappeared, leaving them alone in an apartment. Police and social workers never found the ones who'd abandoned them.

A boy I called "Rabbit" had the look, too. At age ten he'd had to peel his mentally ill mother's hands from his three-year-old sister's neck when the woman tried to strangle her own daughter.

I saw that look every morning when I gazed at the mirror.

But Mother's eyes were worse. There was nothing behind them. She seemed to have no thoughts, no feelings. There was only a blackness spreading into forever.

The skin below those eyes was dark purple, as if she hadn't slept in weeks. She resembled a zombie from a horror movie.

She was in a place I'd never been to. All I could do was stare.

"How are things with you, Robby?" Gigi asked to break the silence.

"I-I'm fine," I stammered.

"And how are you doing, Joyce?" she asked Mother.

We waited. Mother's words emerged slowly from her mouth, as if afraid of what they might find. "O . . . kay. . . . They are trying . . . to fix me. . . . I have to let them . . ."

Gigi leaned forward to hear better. I continued to stare.

"I . . . am . . . on . . . some . . . powerful drugs . . ."

C'mon, I thought impatiently. *Talk normal. Spit it out.*

Gigi encouraged her to go on.

". . . to try . . . to help my brain . . . not have such scattered thoughts."

She slowly reached up with a thin paper napkin and wiped the drool from the corner of her mouth.

Gigi, can't you stop this? I begged silently. *Let's leave!*

"When my brain . . . was moving so fast . . ." Mother frowned as she searched for the next words. "I couldn't think . . . I couldn't hold a job . . . I couldn't take care of myself."

You can't think now, either. Get off the pills! Maybe then you could take care of me like a real mother.

"These drugs make my brain slow down. . . . I have to think . . . about standing up . . . before I stand up."

She hesitated, searching.

"I'm so slow . . . I sound drunk."

Nothing new about that! I thought. *It never bothered you before.*

She bent forward for her glass of water, apparently unsure how far away it was. Finally she reached for it in slow motion. Using both hands to steady it, she raised it to her mouth, sipped, and lowered it back to the table.

The process probably took no more than a minute. It seemed like an hour.

Gigi acted as if nothing unusual was going on. I wanted to bolt and get as far away as I could.

This can't go on much longer, I thought. *She looks exhausted.*

Somehow, though, she seemed to pull herself together and began to sound more normal. "Oh, Robby, my hair . . . is a mess. I don't know if it will ever be pretty again. They put me through e . . . e . . . electroshock therapy . . . several times."

To my surprise, a touch of sadness crossed her face. I hadn't thought she could feel anything at all.

She took a deep breath, then tried to explain.

"The doctors say the brain is made up of millions of cells . . . that transmit our thoughts and feelings." She shrugged. "I don't understand much more than that."

Good! That's more than I need to know. So let's go now!

She wasn't finished. "Some doctors feel my condition . . . is because my brain . . . doesn't function correctly . . . like it has a . . ." She frowned again, searching for a word. "Short circuit . . . and sparks are going off all over the place."

She paused. Gigi and I waited.

"At least that's how I understand it."

Another deep breath, another sigh. Her face became a blank page again.

"When counseling and drugs didn't help . . . they tried e . . . electroshock on my brain."

Suddenly she was looking into a darkness I'd never seen. Her voice rose. "They strap you onto a table. They put straps on your arms and wrists."

The nothingness in her eyes changed to rage. Her breathing grew fast and shallow, as if she'd been running.

"They put straps on your *ankles*, and your *chest*, and put *something—in—your—mouth—so—you—don't—bite—off—your—tongue*!"

She spat the words, as if firing bullets at her past tormentors.

I felt sick to my stomach. Her voice was loud, but I didn't look around to see if the waitress had heard.

"They put a headpiece on. Hooked it up to a generator. Pulled a switch, and sent electricity . . . into my brain." Her voice trailed off.

Gigi and I watched in horror the panic on Mother's trembling, sweating face.

Somehow, I knew she was finished. I reached across the table and held one of her hands.

We sat in silence while she calmed down.

I didn't want to prolong the conversation. But I couldn't help asking, "Did it hurt badly, Mother?"

She raised her shredded napkin to wipe the corner of her lip. I noticed that one side of her mouth was lower than the other.

What did they do to her? How could anyone do this to her?

Still I held her hand. It seemed to strengthen her.

"Pain. Physical pain? I don't think so, Robby. I don't remember anything after they strapped me down. . . . After I woke up, I couldn't function. It was like . . . I had just enough brain to know I was alive, but not enough to make my body do anything. People at the hospital called it . . . 'the conscious dead.' That was pretty much how we felt."

The half hour of listening had drained me, but I had to know one more thing. "Are you better now? Do you think it helped?"

After a long pause, she replied: "I don't know, Robby . . . I don't know."

Gigi decided we'd all had enough for one day. "Robby, dear," she said in an overly cheerful voice, "please ask the waitress for the check so your mother can pay for our meal and we can walk her home."

That was my cue to leave the table so that Gigi could slip Mother some money. I played along; it seemed important to them, I thought, so why spoil it?

When we got back to her apartment, Gigi asked if I wanted to talk.

"No, thank you. I can't talk about it now. Maybe later."

Talk? I couldn't talk. I could barely think. I needed time to sort out my feelings. I knew the mental pictures of this visit would remain with me forever.

Most of the time I'd hated my mother. But on that day I just felt sick. All at once I'd realized that maybe she didn't have control over her actions. She was obviously in a battle to survive—day by day, hour by hour, minute by minute.

My stomach churned. Sympathy began to compete with the anger that was always there.

But the anger was stronger. Mother had ruined Gigi's life and helped to destroy my father's. And in my 13-year-old mind, none of that compared to what she had done to me.

For months after that day, I couldn't sort things out. Sympathy fought for a place in my heart. It seemed the lion of anger might have to live alongside the lamb of sympathy.

Then came the day when Mother resolved the conflict.

Junior high graduation in Princeton was a major event. Pomp and circumstance made the day so important that even Art and Fran, two of Gigi's relatives, drove in from Rockford that spring of 1968. They arrived with Gigi in time for handshakes and kisses before the ceremony.

I was peacock proud as I sat on the stage in my secondhand suit and tie. Suddenly, though, a familiar voice rang from the back of the auditorium.

"Yoo-hoo! Robby!"

It was Mother, staggering drunkenly toward the front.

Gigi rose quickly, meeting her in the aisle. Mother was steered to the back of the room.

I can't believe this! What is she doing here? How can she do this to me?

I hate her. . . . I hate her. . . . I hate her!

When the time came for me to accept my diploma, I didn't walk with head held high. I slumped my shoulders and looked at the floor, hoping against hope that Mother wouldn't embarrass me again.

But as I reached for that prized piece of paper, her voice broke the respectful silence.

"Yeah, Robby!" she yelled. "Whoopee!"

People shifted in their seats as uncomfortable laughter spread through the auditorium. I wanted to drop through the floor.

When the program was over, I wished I could disappear. None of the other kids or their parents came to congratulate me.

Gigi, Art, Fran, and I milled around outside as Mother hung all over me. The smell of booze on her breath was nauseating. I wanted to scream at her, to smash her face in.

Most of all, I wanted her to shut up and leave me alone forever.

And in that moment, the lion of my anger shredded the lamb of my sympathy.

/14/

A Few Good Men

"GET THAT WOMAN OUT OF my *life*!" I yelled in my next counseling session.

Marv's thick eyebrows drew together as he took the blast.

"She ruined my graduation. She's caused me nothing but pain since the day I was born. I hate her, I hate her, I hate her!"

"Now, Robby," Marv began.

I wasn't about to listen to his platitudes. "No more!" I raged. "I don't want to see her anymore—ever."

Marv, a good man with a gentle heart, let me rant and rave without comment. Finally he excused me from the session.

After that explosion, the Big Boys staff must have feared I would hurt myself or someone else. Within days they took the chemistry set away from me, increased the frequency of my counseling sessions to weekly, and banned Mother from the property. No one mentioned another trip to Chicago to see her; it was a good thing no one tried.

When I was younger, Gigi's weekly visits had helped to calm me down. But she was 74 now, and the trip was too difficult for her. Every couple of months a staff member would take me to visit her, but I missed her more than I could say. She was the only one whose opinion kept me from getting into real trouble. Her visits had deposited enough love in my emotional storehouse to keep me on track, but with fewer and fewer deposits my reserves were almost gone.

Six months after the graduation episode, Gigi asked me to go with her to Mother's halfway house. I went because she asked me to, but had no reaction when I saw my mother. I'd tuned her out; she'd become merely one more person from my past.

Nobody seemed to realize it, but I'd moved on. Mother wasn't joining me on my trip into the future.

It appeared that with the possible exception of Gigi, nobody else from my family was, either.

I especially needed a dad at this stage, but mine would never be able to play that role. Fortunately, some other men came into my life and cared enough to try to make a difference.

Jim was a man of few words and no conversation.

When I was in junior high, he became the Big Boys houseparent. Less than six feet tall but incredibly strong from years of working in Nevada silver mines, he taught me how to lift weights.

In my case, weight lifting wasn't just exercise. It helped me blow off steam, and Jim seemed to know that.

He also tried hard to divert my anger in positive directions, teaching me Morse code and helping me to become a ham radio operator. He and another local man showed me how to build my own radio from a kit.

My self-esteem soared when I created a radio that worked. So did my pride when other operators treated me as one of them.

Using the call letters WN9UHJ, I kept radio logs and swapped postcards with operators from all over the world. Nobody knew who I was or where I was transmitting from.

I could just be me. It was awesome to finally not be called "a kid from the Home."

For two years, Swaney was a substitute houseparent on weekends, on days off, and during vacations. He was a master woodcraftsman, too, with an easygoing, lovable golden retriever personality that made it hard to harass him too much.

Built like a bowling pin topped with thinning, sandy-red hair, Swaney always had a smile and a joke for us. Even our hardened hearts were touched to know that he'd married his wife, Anna, knowing that she had cancer. They would have only a few years together, but he cared for her each day.

A man of courage, Swaney dared to take seven of us on a week-long canoe trip in upper Minnesota. In the Boundary Waters wilderness we paddled lakes, carried canoes and camp gear over portages, drank from unpolluted springs, and camped on islands at night. We fought, caught, cleaned, and cooked ferocious freshwater muskie. We bled when huge deer flies swarmed and bit ten times worse than mosquitoes. We swam, then jerked leeches off our bodies.

Swaney was outnumbered by us rowdies. That six-day adventure must have taxed all of his patience and skill.

His influence went beyond outdoorsmanship. One day he

pulled me aside and, without embarrassment, talked to me about sex. "God designed sex as an act of love that blesses a loving marriage," he told me. "It should be seen as a gift from God that is only used after a man and woman have married."

This was news to me. The older boys at the Home viewed girls only as potential "scores"—an idea reinforced by their supply of dirty magazines and novels. In fact, pornography had been my main reading material since I'd arrived on Big Boys in sixth grade.

As a hot-blooded teenager with few moral restraints, I didn't buy Swaney's point of view. I doubted I ever would.

It was hard not to respect him, though. And I couldn't help picking up his love of the wilderness.

Bob was a caseworker, substitute houseparent, conservationist, master bowman, and hunter.

Sporting buzz-cut hair, he was lean like an army Ranger. Though I wasn't one of his counseling clients, he went out of his way for me.

When I was in high school, Bob taught me how to load and aim a rifle. He took me hunting for rabbit, squirrel, and deer, then showed me how to skin, clean, and prepare the meat.

He also demonstrated how to tell time and position from the sun, move quietly through the woods, and find my direction without a compass. I learned to spend many peaceful hours in the fields and woods, the quiet and outdoor smells feeding my soul.

The greatest lesson Bob taught me, though, came when he took three of us teenage boys elk hunting near Iron River in northern Michigan.

We'd searched for days without seeing a single elk. Early in the morning on the last day of our trip, we were walking a dirt logging trail through dense forest. Suddenly Bob turned left, raised his bow, and froze.

A huge bull elk with a magnificent set of antlers stood in a clearing. I was so excited I could hardly breathe.

Bulls usually travel alone, but two cows and several calves were with this one. We knew that if he bolted, he might make it into the woods to safety, but the cows and calves would be fair game.

The bull stood his ground, slowly raising his elegant head and staring as if to say, "You'll have to shoot me first and give my cows and calves a chance to get away."

We boys had our guns aimed at the cows, safeties off. For what seemed an eternity, we waited for Bob. He'd made it clear that we were to shoot only after he let his first arrow fly.

But nothing happened. *What is he waiting for?* I thought.

At last he slowly relaxed the bowstring and lowered the bow. Confused, we clicked on our safeties and lowered our rifles. The bull signaled with his tail; the cows and calves bolted into the woods. Finally the majestic animal himself turned and walked away.

Bob never said a word as he walked past us and headed down the long trail to the car. Later, when we stopped for a drink and a snack, he finally offered an explanation.

"Boys, we came to hunt elk," he said.

We nodded.

"We reached our goal," he continued. "We found that elk. In

fact, we found a trophy buck. Whether or not that buck's head is hanging on a wall somewhere makes no difference. We will always know if we had fired, we had him dead to rights."

He paused, then added a phrase I'd heard him say before: "We don't have to shoot them all."

After letting us digest that, he added, "That buck's incredible courage and selfless attitude saved him. He could have bolted and probably saved his own life. Instead he chose to remain as the prime target so the others could survive."

"Can you believe it?" one of the guys exclaimed. "That was the most awesome thing I've ever seen."

"It was an excellent example of the biblical message, 'No greater love has a man than he lay down his life for a friend,'" Bob concluded. Then he picked up his bow and started down the trail again.

We went home without a trophy, but with a memory that would stick with us forever.

Late that night, I thought about the kind of love Bob had talked about. Except for maybe Gigi, I couldn't imagine anyone ever caring enough to lay down his or her life for anyone—especially not for me.

Finally, there was Marv.

Already my caseworker, he was beginning to become something more—something I couldn't put a term to and wasn't willing to admit anyway.

With our usual juvenile sarcasm, we guys had labeled him "Arvey Dog"—after cartoon character Underdog, who always came to the rescue in a bumbling way. Marv was, of course, much smarter than we were ready to acknowledge.

With patience and bravery, Marv taught me how to drive his Plymouth—a unique vehicle with a push-button gear changer. He also fought valiantly to guide me through the stormy waters of adolescence.

Marv's biggest challenge was a struggle that had haunted me for years.

After wondering what I'd done that had made my parents decide not to raise me, I had come to an uneasy acceptance that they were the problem. But there was still the question of my destiny, a question I finally asked Marv during our counseling sessions.

"Am I doomed to be crazy like my mother and father?"

It was no idle query. Much as I wanted to be a survivor and live a normal life, I still felt no genuine hope for my future.

"Am I genetically programmed to be like my parents?" I asked Marv more than once. "Is my brain going to misfire like my mother's does? Should I try to get ready to be crazy? Will I live my life on the streets, in halfway houses and mental hospitals?"

Marv worked hard to convince me that the story of my life didn't have to be a replay of my parents' actions and reactions. Even when I threw Pauline's wackiness into the stew, he insisted my future could be different from my past.

"You're not doomed to be like your parents or Pauline, Robby," he assured me. "But you do have to learn how to deal with life and control your frustration and anger. You have to stop thinking bad things are going to happen and look forward to all that is waiting for you. There's a good life ahead of you, but only if you choose to accept it."

It was so hard to believe. I couldn't touch the future. I didn't dare hope; every hope of my childhood had been smashed. There was no proof that Marv knew what he was talking about.

One day I asked him, "How can someone believe in a hope they can't see?"

Marv sighed, then tried a different approach.

"Okay, Robby. What if you're right? What if you *are* doomed to be just like your parents? What are you going to do then?"

He sat back in his chair, probably thinking he'd shocked me into silence.

No one had ever bothered to ask me that question, but I had an answer. Looking straight through him, without emotion, I said, "I'd get myself fixed so no kid of mine will ever go through what I've had to."

A stunned Marv had no response.

Session over.

15

The Rebel

As I walked through the high school halls as a freshman in the fall of 1968, my "I don't care" attitude sat solidly on one shoulder; its cousin, "Don't mess with me," sat on the other.

The junior high caste system had left me with a contempt that alienated me from even the kids I liked. We "Homies" just couldn't break into the good social circles no matter how hard we tried.

A girl I'd liked in eighth grade told me she couldn't be my girlfriend because her dad didn't like kids from the Home. So I'd just stopped trying. No way was this kid going to beg to be included.

Snide comments and sideways looks in the hallways and lunchroom irritated me, but I stuffed the anger and walked by the offenders as if I didn't know they existed. *I don't care about these snobs,* I told myself. *They're stupid, cruel, and insignificant. They can't hurt me if I don't let them, and I won't!*

Isolating myself soothed the pain of rejection, but it didn't calm the rage. My defiance was an open invitation to fight. It gave me a reason to explode and hurt some guy who might think he could take me on.

Sports became an outlet for my pent-up emotions and hormonal energy. Cross-country, basketball, and track helped blow out the stress. I finally felt part of something, too; even being a cog in a small machine felt good.

After running the mile in less than five minutes, I qualified to compete at the district level. What a lift that was—until a skinny, troublemaking upperclassman and his strong, silent sidekick cornered me in the locker room the day before the spring meet.

"Hey, hotshot," Mouth yelled as he pushed me up against a locker. "I don't care what the stopwatch says; you're not good enough to be on this team. You think you're some superstar, but you're not. It's time someone takes that chip off your shoulder."

I could tell he intended to be that someone, so I tried to stare him down. "You're in for a good red-belly," he announced with a sneer, grabbing me and trying to twist me around.

Avoiding a red-belly was worth all the effort I could muster. I knew from experience that it meant getting my abdomen slapped so hard that the skin would turn scarlet and welt up. The pain would feel like fire.

I struggled until Goon, the sidekick, grabbed my arms and pinned them behind my back. As Mouth pulled up my shirt, I backpedaled into Goon, who stumbled into the lockers behind him. Raising both legs, I used him for leverage, ramming my feet into Mouth's chest. He slammed into a row of lockers, denting them and knocking the wind out of his lungs.

Twisting Goon to the floor, I landed on top of him. I kicked at

Mouth as my head banged Goon's into the floor, but Goon wouldn't let go. Mouth finally sat on my legs, pinning me.

Outnumbered and outsized, I lost the battle. I got the worst red-belly of my life; it hurt for days.

I felt some satisfaction, though, when I overheard Mouth complaining about his sore ribs and watched Goon pop aspirin for his week-long headache. The word went out: *If you want Mitchell, you'd better bring at least three guys.*

These Townies didn't seem to understand that I wasn't some ordinary kid they could push around. For years I'd lived with bullies who were worse. My message was loud and clear: *Just give me the slightest reason to hurt you, and I won't hold back.*

Mouth never could get three or more upperclassmen together to finish the job he and Goon had started. Soon I seemed surrounded by a cloud of my own making that pushed even nice kids away.

Playing sports, while giving me an emotional outlet, caused a different kind of pain.

When we had out-of-town games or track meets, our team returned to the school late, sometimes after 11 P.M. Many athletes' parents would be waiting; other Townies drove their own cars and offered friends a ride. Never included by either group, we "Homies" tried to slip away quickly so it wasn't obvious that no one was waiting for us.

John Smith, a nice guy with an amazingly accurate long-distance shot, was the sophomore basketball coach. He had his hands full with me. I had enough talent to start or come off the bench as the sixth man, but my aggressive, combative, cocky attitude didn't fit his gentlemanly style of play.

It didn't help that many of the other players' parents didn't care for me. Adults in our conservative farming town didn't appreciate my "rebellious" 1960s hairstyle. Several called me a "long-haired hippie ruffian" to my face. Not only did they want me off the starting team—they wanted me off the squad entirely.

My response: letting my hair grow to shoulder length like my irreverent basketball idol, Pistol Pete Maravich. As I expected, that really ticked the men off. I enjoyed irritating these people who wouldn't let me date their daughters or even let their sons hang out with me.

"Bench him 'til he cuts that hair!" someone usually yelled at the games.

"Put a *good* boy in there," another voice would call from the other side of the court.

One man walked up to me after a game with a dollar bill in his hand. "Here, kid," he said with a sneer. "Take this and get a haircut."

Looking him in the eye, I answered, "You can give me the buck, mister, but I'm not cutting my hair." Thrusting the dollar back in his pocket, he stalked off in a huff.

Some teammates weren't on my side, either. Two of the starters were nice guys and just urged me to "tone it down," but two others hated my guts. The feeling was mutual. They didn't want me on the team, and their parents made that known—loudly.

No matter how tough I tried to seem, the jeers hurt. The most painful of all came from the cheerleaders.

They often opened a game by cheering for the coach: "Yeah, rah, John!" Then each cheerleader would add the name of a starter. But in the first three games I started, the cheerleader who should have yelled my name substituted the name of a player she thought *should* have started.

"Why don't you call out, 'Yeah, rah, Robby'?" I asked the girl after the third time she did this.

"You shouldn't be *playing*, much less *starting*," she snapped, turning and walking away.

Despite the catcalls, I stuck with it. But when I made the varsity team in my junior year, what should have been a source of pride that fall of 1970 became a nightmare.

Mouth, the red-belly tormentor, was a senior now. He still hated my guts and made sure the other guys did, too.

The varsity coach and I clashed daily. Talent got me on the team, but my attitude made him want to break me. Often he'd make me do twice as many drills as the other guys. Things got so bad that some players couldn't stand to watch as this man rode my case.

Sure, I had an attitude problem. But it was clear that the coach was trying to make my life so miserable that I'd quit.

The only one who truly understood me was Paul, a fellow resident at the Home. He had come to Little Boys when he was eight and I was nine.

Paul was into football and wrestling, so in the fall and winter we often walked a mile or so back to the Home together. "He's just abusing you," Paul would say of the coach during those walks. "Why don't you quit? You don't need this garbage."

"Yeah, I know," I'd answer. "But there's no way I'm going to let Coach have the pleasure of breaking me. I'll show him I'm no quitter. I can stick it out as long as he can."

It was cold, walking back to the Home on those winter

evenings. Sometimes I'd glance through the picture windows of two-story, wooden houses on Euclid Street. I'd see real families at dinner tables, smiling and eating, enjoying and understanding a sense of acceptance and belonging.

By now it was obvious that was something I would never find.

/16/

A Losing Season

THE HOLIDAY SEASON OF MY junior year was, as usual, bittersweet.

Christmas music and a decorated tree in the dining hall perked the place up. Television specials, school performances, and programs the staff dragged us to at church provided a change of pace. But all these things screamed *happy, happy, happy—family, family, family.*

Even though kids like us enjoyed the entertainment, we often spent long, dark nights afterward struggling with loneliness.

Several church groups visited during December. They staged programs, sang carols, and even played basketball with the older boys in our small gym.

We liked beating these Townies and gladly accepted the presents. But most of us older kids wanted to ask, "Where are you people the rest of the year? For eleven months we're outcasts, and then all of a sudden we're special? Don't you think you could take turns so we'd have visitors at least once a month throughout the year?"

I didn't ask this out loud. With only a year and a half before graduation and entry into the real world, this issue didn't matter to me anymore. Besides, I could remember how, when I'd lived on Little Boys, holiday visits had been a treat. I didn't want to ruin Christmas for the current little kids who needed the attention.

Christmas meant presents, too. But now that I had some money and could afford a nice gift for Gigi, I didn't feel free to buy her one. As I'd become richer, she'd become poorer. The holiday season stretched her budget because she not only paid for the gift she gave me but also for the one Mother supposedly sent.

I knew Gigi would be embarrassed if my gift to her cost more than the one she gave me. So I would buy her a lace handkerchief or dime-store perfume. She always raved over it as if it were the very thing she'd asked Santa for.

Still, it felt good to have a stash of hard-earned cash to draw from. Some of the other kids didn't have a cent to their names. They couldn't buy even a simple trinket for the people they loved. Such poverty at Christmas added one more blow to their fragile self-esteem.

When children at the Home talked about wanting to give a gift, it was always intended for a mother or grandmother. Fathers were nearly nonexistent for most kids like us; the few dads who surfaced were usually pathetic.

I didn't give any of the younger kids money to buy a present. If I had, 60 pairs of empty hands would have reached out instantly. Since I couldn't fill that many, I didn't fill even one.

The counselors tried hard to see that none of us would have to stay at the Home for Christmas Eve and Christmas morning. When they exhausted all leads in a child's extended family, they persuaded area households to take kids in. I thought such kids would have been better off staying at the Home with each other, not feeling as if they were butting in on someone else's family celebration.

As for me, I spent my holidays with Gigi. That helped me through a season that was tough for kids like us.

Another adult was beginning to affect my life, too.

Dave had come to us right out of college, literally wearing a white shirt and conservative tie. He spouted classroom theories on how to help us poor juvenile delinquents.

I'd seen guys like Dave come and go. Some were studying for their master's degrees in social work, and we were their field project. Many were just marking time. Others were dodging the draft to avoid fighting in Vietnam.

Usually raised in comfortable homes by caring parents, these guys had never experienced our degree of unmet financial, physical, or emotional needs. They were totally unprepared for our hostility. Despite their sincere attempts to help us, we quickly chewed most of them up and spit them out—then cheered at the rush of power we felt when they left.

Another new white shirt, I snickered when Dave arrived. *We'll give him a ride for his money. He doesn't have a chance.*

Dave was smaller than many of us on Big Boys. Standing about 5'10", he weighed around 142 pounds and wore glasses that always seemed to be trying to slip off his nose.

We also thought he was absolutely clueless. Some of us placed bets on whether we could run him out in record time. Most of us put our money on less than a month.

Motivated by the jackpot, we heaped serious verbal abuse on the poor man. By the end of his first week, he was in shock. The university social work program hadn't taught him how to cope with the kind of anger and disrespect being thrown at him.

I'm sure he wanted to yell, "Hey, guys, I'm here to help you! Give me a break!" But there were no breaks on our turf; not only were we ungrateful, we were downright malicious.

Somehow Dave hung in there. Within a couple of weeks, we saw a change. Clearly he'd decided to survive our abuse. Maybe he'd developed a fascination with us—something like people feel when they see a car crash, horrified but unable to look away.

More likely, though, he simply dug his feet in and set himself a goal. He seemed determined to try to understand us. We had our own culture, and he was the outsider trying to fit in.

Those of us who bet we could drive Dave out in a month or less lost our money. He stayed, consistently and honestly demonstrating that he truly cared. He earned our grudging respect—and showed me that not all adults were fakes.

Despite Dave's influence, though, I found myself getting into trouble. With basketball season over, I had too much free time. There was nothing to push the dark shadows away.

Church activities didn't do the job. Church attendance was enforced on Sunday morning and at youth group on Sunday evening, but had little effect on me. I spent most of the time trying to get a girl in a dark corner for a quick kiss, or being a smart aleck to make the adults miserable.

Soon I was pushing further down the antisocial, careless path. I began dabbling in alcohol and marijuana. I never bought any "weed," but another guy did. We smoked together whenever we could.

I probably would have dipped deeper into drugs if I hadn't been so afraid of being caught. The 24 hours I'd endured in Chicago's Audy Home when I was 8 was a nightmare I didn't want to repeat—ever.

Trying drugs was partly rebellion, but also an effort to dull briefly the ache in my heart. And the ache was growing worse. Like many boys I knew, I was beginning to think, *I hurt. I see no relief to this hurt. If I have to hurt like this, then other people are going to have to hurt as well.*

I didn't want to cross that line. But I was slowly losing the fight.

By the end of my junior year, the river of my life was flowing aimlessly through deep canyons of despair. Nothing seemed worth caring about anymore.

Those canyon walls kept me from seeing that hope hadn't given up on me—and was planning something I never could have imagined.

/17/

The Lifeguard

When the summer before my senior year rolled around, I finally got some good news. Somehow I'd managed to get hired as a lifeguard and swim instructor at Covenant Harbor, a church camp at Lake Geneva, Wisconsin.

I'd been to the camp before; all of us "Homey" kids spent a week of each summer there, doing things like learning to swim and sitting through Bible studies. The latter hadn't made much of an impact on me, but the former had helped prepare me for this summer job. So had hanging around the Princeton pool and canoeing with Swaney and the guys.

Now it was my turn to be a lifeguard and swim instructor to other kids.

This is gonna be great! I thought. *A whole summer away from the Home to chase girls!*

To say I was excited by that prospect would be an understatement. Bob the hunter had mentioned that females of many species put off a scent when they're ready for male attention. I didn't know whether human girls put off a scent, but I did know that some—when away from their parents—let it be known they were interested in a bit of romancing. I was always on the hunt for those.

The camp staff wasn't used to someone with such rough edges. While they didn't ship me back to the Home, they didn't put up with me being a lowlife either.

"We don't use language like that," the girls on the staff told me. "We like to laugh, Robby, but not at dirty jokes."

Their message was clear: Step out of line and you're in trouble. That irritated me; after all, it would slow down my summer agenda.

Still, I enjoyed working with the kids. Each Sunday about a hundred arrived and were assigned to cabins holding eight kids and one counselor. Some weeks were for elementary school-age campers, some for junior high kids, and some for high school students.

Daytime activities included arts and crafts and sports. I stayed busy giving swimming lessons from early morning through mid-afternoon, being a lifeguard, and teaching canoeing and sailing.

Evenings weren't without fun, but Bible studies, speakers, and group singing seemed to occupy most of the time. I began to feel uncomfortable. Most of the camp workers were calm, happy, full of hope—traits alien to my world.

The college-age counselors were excited about "spiritual growth" and looked forward to their futures. They were walking, talking examples of what I wasn't. Their positive view of life attracted me, but my defenses and arrogance brushed that aside.

Of course they're excited about life, I grumbled. *Why wouldn't they be? None of them live in an orphanage and have crazy parents.*

Any interest I might have had in exploring spiritual things disappeared the moment a blonde daughter of a minister showed up for a week of volunteer work. My eyes bugged out, my blood pumped, and my hormones went into high gear.

Some female staff members sensed I was on the prowl. "He's a wolf," they warned the girl. "Don't trust him."

One night several of them ambushed me. "Listen up, Buster," their leader threatened, wagging her finger in front of my nose. "Do anything out of line and we'll personally see that you fry."

Like I cared! My target was only going to be here for a week. I'd locked her in my sights, and the hunt was on.

In spite of the warnings, this girl didn't brush me off. She hadn't sent out "I want to fool around" signals, but I was convinced she'd be an easy catch.

Once we spent a little time together, though, I realized that wasn't the case. Even though she'd been warned, she didn't seem to feel a bit uncomfortable around me. She had qualities I'd never seen before in anyone. Her incredible sense of peace amazed me. And it was obvious she knew who she was and didn't feel threatened.

This is weird, I thought. Any girl in her right mind would know my motives weren't pure. Why hadn't she rejected me?

We kissed at times, but I found myself unwilling to try anything more. I'd never cared about a girl's reputation before—or mine, either. Her innocence turned my plans upside down.

The day before she left, we paddled a canoe on the lake and talked. Then she said, "Tell me about your relationship with Jesus."

I mumbled a vague sentence or two, then stopped. I wasn't going to lie to her. "I don't have one," I admitted. "I don't believe in Jesus. Life and God have abandoned me and left me to do the best I can on my own."

I expected her to be shocked and disappointed; she wasn't. I expected her to turn cold and tell me to take her to shore; she didn't. Instead, she listened calmly as I cautiously told her a little about my childhood.

When I finished, she said quietly, "Maybe if you allow God into your life, you will find the peace you don't have now."

I protested. "That's easy for you to say. You have parents who care for you. Compared to what I've been through, your life has been a picnic."

"God cares for all people, no matter what the circumstances," she replied. "I know you've had it tough, but we're promised a better way if we trust Him."

"Yeah," I muttered, turning the canoe toward shore.

Saying good-bye the next day broke my heart. I wanted more of this girl and the peace she seemed to offer.

For weeks her words haunted me. *Could it be true? Could God really care about somebody like me?* The evidence I'd collected didn't seem to be in His favor.

Am I missing something? I wondered. She clearly had a peace I didn't have. So did most of the staff members. *But they come from a different world. I'm not good enough to be in that world.*

I remembered something she'd told me. "God forgave Moses, David, and Paul, even though each of them murdered someone. He'll forgive anyone who honestly asks to be forgiven, no matter what they've done."

If God could forgive those guys, maybe He'll forgive me for all the bad things I've done, I thought. *At least I haven't murdered anyone yet.*

I wrestled with those issues for the rest of the summer, but didn't discuss them with the camp staff. This was a personal journey. I didn't want to be overwhelmed by anyone's enthusiastic attempts to "save" me.

When I returned to the Home that fall of 1971, I was surprised to find that, for the first time, my bedroom had been split into two smaller, private ones. As a senior, I finally had a room of my own with a bureau—and all the drawers were mine.

The silence and privacy took some getting used to. But I was going to need it.

/18/

Are You Real?

For years we kids from the Home had been hauled to Sunday school and church in Princeton. Nola had read us Bible stories. Prayer had been said at each meal. But none of it had seemed important to me.

It all sounded like a boring history lesson or a bunch of stories with no connection to my life. I was more interested in the teen activities and seeing whether I could get the girls to giggle during the church service.

But, now, after meeting a girl my age who actually spoke and acted like someone I wished I could be like, I thought maybe it was time to read seriously some of the "Jesus chapters" she'd talked about. In my newly private room I could pick up the Bible I'd stuffed into the bottom drawer—and read it without having to defend myself or tune out the sarcastic comments of roommates.

As I began to read, several things jumped out at me.

This guy got hungry, thirsty, and tired. He even got His feet dirty. I'd never thought about that.

He was let down by those He trusted. I could relate.

Then I read a verse that knocked my socks off. *This man said He is God.*

He had some nerve. He wasn't just claiming to understand God, or to be one of God's children. He was claiming to be God.

Apparently that claim was so offensive to the religious leaders of the day that they set up a plan to have Him killed. I'd had it rough, but at least no one had put out a contract on me.

When Dave, the "white shirt" who'd hung in there, recognized my new interest, he loaned me a book called *Mere Christianity* by C. S. Lewis. "The author was an intellectual giant and an atheist before he became a Christian," Dave said. "You might like to follow his logical reasoning as he investigates this stuff."

I discovered that after much research and reflection, Lewis had decided that an intelligent seeker must come to one of three conclusions: Either Jesus was a lunatic or lied about being God—or was really who He claimed to be.

It seemed that, like Lewis, I was being forced to make a black-or-white decision. There was no gray area; I was either with this Jesus or against Him.

The Man said He was God. If this is true, I'd better pay attention. If He isn't, then everything else He said has to be the ranting of a nut case like Mother.

I already knew there was no reason to try to learn anything from a lunatic.

I went back to the Bible and kept reading.

It surprised me that Jesus got angry. Getting mad was a feeling I knew well. But His anger wasn't like mine.

We both got angry at hypocrisy; I liked that. He got frustrated at people; so did I. But His frustration wasn't caused by things that were done to Him. It was caused by people who didn't even want to consider what God's plan for them might be.

I wasn't sure there was a heavenly blueprint for me. But I had to admit that if there was a Creator of the universe, it might be wise to find out whether He had a plan—and, if so, to follow it.

I saw that Jesus talked often about eternal life. I was more worried about living past 20. Yet I couldn't help but wonder: *If there's more to come, including eternity, might there really be hope for me if I change?*

Jesus said the Spirit of God could come into my heart and change me. *How can something like the Spirit of God fit into my body, into my heart? How can I believe in something I can't see or touch?*

That argument rolled around inside me for a couple of days. Then a thought began to dawn on me. I had a physical body that already contained three parts I couldn't see—intellect, emotions, and will. My intellect often told me I wasn't smart enough to go to college; my emotions said a kid from an orphanage didn't deserve to go to college; yet my will fought back, insisting that I would go to college, succeed, and become more than my childhood.

So if intellect, emotions, and will that are invisible and untouchable but very, very real can live within a kid like me, then is it possible that maybe—just maybe—the Spirit of God can also live inside me?

It was all tough to understand. The concepts racing in my brain started to bump into each other. I needed a sounding board to help me sort things out.

Dave helped steer me through the muddle. He let me ramble and didn't preach or teach. He listened, every now and then raising a question for me to think about. At times my brain seemed to hurt from working so hard.

I kept reading, noting that Jesus said thieves come to steal, kill, and destroy—while He came so we can have "abundant" life. Stealing, killing, destroying—all were familiar. For me, any sense of a normal childhood had been stolen and destroyed; any hope for a normal future had been killed long ago.

But was Jesus actually offering me—and other bitter, angry people—hope for a better life today? It sounded outrageous.

After all, my prospects weren't promising. In less than a year the Home's staff would hand me a one-way bus ticket to the place of my choice, along with their best wishes. That was it.

The idea of being on my own with no immediate family or financial safety net looked pretty scary. College was a possibility, but I didn't see it as a golden key to the good life. Both my parents had gone to college, and their lives stank.

All I knew was that I had to find a way to escape the cycle of failure that had trapped other boys from the Home. I really wanted to believe I could rise above my bizarre childhood. *Could this Jesus really change things?*

When I got to Bible sections about Jesus healing the crippled, blind, and deaf, I usually passed them over. *That sure doesn't apply to me,* I thought. *I'm a three-sport athlete!* But one day Dave brought me up short.

"Hasn't life maybe crippled you emotionally, Robby?" he asked. "Are you perhaps like the hardheaded people you've been reading about? Is it possible your pride has blinded you to the promises of God? Is your fear to trust making you deaf to those at camp who said Jesus made a difference in their lives?"

I asked for time to think about his uncomfortable questions.

The camp staff members really were different, I admitted. *Maybe*

I should have listened to what they had to say instead of dismissing them because of their easy childhoods.

In our next session I told Dave I didn't have answers yet. "What else should I think about?" I asked.

"Tell me, Robby, how do you explain the guys who ran closest to Jesus and then watched Him die on the cross? They buried His body and then claimed to have seen Him rise from that grave, just like He promised. Nearly every one of those men was later tortured and killed for telling everyone who would listen to them that Jesus had risen from the dead."

I shrugged. "I don't know if they were lying, Dave. But I sure couldn't find 11 guys like me who'd go through torture and a horrible death just to play some trick on the world."

Dave nodded. "Did you read about the more than 500 who claimed they saw Him after He rose from the grave? They weren't close friends or disciples. They were just ordinary people. But what they saw, heard, and felt inside really must have changed them."

When I didn't answer, he let me stew for a while. "Just keep at it, Robby. We all face this decision sometime in our lives. And we have to face it alone."

At our next session, I told Dave, "I know if a kid disobeys his parent, that kid should apologize and ask for forgiveness. And I know I've said and done things that the Bible says are wrong. But I can't figure out why I should apologize to a God who's never been there for my parents or for me."

Dave thought for a while before he responded. "Is it possible that your parents were hard-hearted and too proud to turn to God for help? And that maybe your pride and anger have hardened your heart, too? You've been hurt so many times you're afraid to trust."

Then he asked a question that hurt: "Could it be that your view of your own biological father is so poor that you are closed to the idea of God as a spiritual Father?"

Something was trying to open the locked doors of my heart. This stuff wasn't safe. Fighting to keep the doors closed, I said I needed more time to think.

What Dave said tumbled around in my head for days. Finally I realized that it all boiled down to one issue.

What am I going to decide about this Jesus? Am I going to reject Him as a lunatic like my mother, or risk reaching out one more time for hope and accept Him as who He says He is?

On a September afternoon in 1971, at age 17, I made a decision.

In a little bedroom too small to turn my bed around in, I got down on my knees. *Jesus,* I prayed, *if You are real, come into my nightmare. Forgive me of my sins and change me.*

If You really change me, I'm Yours forever.

If You don't, You're a fraud and a joke.

Not exactly the kind of prayer evangelist Billy Graham would have suggested.

I didn't hear angel choirs singing. I didn't fall down and roll around on the floor in spiritual ecstasy.

But somehow I knew that despite my weak faith, in that moment, the God of the universe had reached deep into my heart and something had changed.

For the first time in years, I couldn't wait to see what was coming next.

/19/

A New Beginning

IF THIS WAS A FRESH start, I wasn't sure I liked it.

For one thing, fighting was still a problem. The pecking order on Big Boys awarded top-dog status to the toughest guy; as a senior who was stronger than his peers, I shouldn't have been challenged by anyone in his right mind. But some of my fellow "inmates" weren't in their right minds.

Occasionally one in particular would test me. Instead of beating him up, I'd tickle him until he cried "Uncle." At least with tickling, my opponent wasn't sore for a week or two.

Unfortunately, that wasn't enough for another guy. He was strong, angry, and wanted to be top dog. He baited me regularly.

One day we got into a heated argument that wound up in a face-to-face screaming match. I could tell he ached for me to take that first swing so he wouldn't be blamed for the result.

I was eager to teach him a lesson. The "old" me couldn't wait to feel his flesh on my fist. As with Ralph and Jack at Castle Rock in *Lord of the Flies,* someone was gonna get hurt.

Suddenly, though, I remembered the words of Jesus: "Turn the other cheek." I found myself spinning around and walking away. Storming into my room, I slammed the door, unhappy because no blood was dripping off my enemy's face. Grabbing my Bible, I flung it across the room.

I just missed a chance to pound that idiot and prove who's boss! Am I a fool for not smashing his face in? I need an answer right now! Speak to me!

The Bible landed on my bed, open and upside down. *Upside down? I wonder if that's my answer.* I hoped to find an angry passage that said something like, "Go out and slay a thousand people and let their blood run in the fields."

I flipped the book over. Then I read a verse: "A gentle answer turns away wrath."

That's not what I wanted to hear.

I'd been beaten, put down, and embarrassed before, but rarely humbled. Reading this 3,000-year-old proverb about the wisdom of gentleness and self-control was a humbling experience.

My anger began to evaporate. *Maybe this stuff isn't dusty history at all. Maybe it's practical today, even for a guy like me.*

Throwing a Bible down and screaming at God might not be a good idea, I guessed, but it seemed to me that this proverb hadn't appeared by accident. Apparently God did care and was sending a message.

Our relationship grew stronger that day. I began to believe that the Creator of the universe really did know me and was willing to show me a better way—if I gave this stuff a chance.

My life seemed to be starting fresh in another way, too. Early that spring of 1972, Guilford College accepted me as a student for the fall semester.

Gigi and I had discussed this possibility before. Now I surprised her when I said, "It will be easier and definitely cheaper to go to school in Chicago with some friends from church camp."

She listened as I listed all the negatives of going to North Carolina. "The scholarship to Guilford only includes tuition, so I'm going to have to pay for room, board, supplies, travel, and miscellaneous expenses. The monthly Social Security check I get because of my father's disability, added to my nest egg in the stock market, will help some. But I'll still have to work at least 20 hours a week and scrimp to cover costs.

"And I'll be too far away from you, Gigi."

Then it was my turn to be surprised. "I want you to go to Guilford for at least one year, Robby," she said firmly. "Go for me. If you hate it after that year, we'll find some way for you to go to college here in Illinois."

I was taken aback. Gigi had never asked me to do anything major like this, just for her. How could I say no?

She was right. The distance wouldn't affect our relationship. At 78 she was already too fragile to travel to Princeton, so we talked regularly on the phone. I visited her in Chicago every couple of months, sometimes reporting on the awkward once- or twice-a-year lunches with Mother that Gigi urged me to have. I always told her Mother was doing okay, even though she wasn't. The only change going to Guilford would bring would be spending more on long-distance phoning and travel.

Even though I hated to go so far away and wished I could be

with my new church and camp friends, I finally agreed it would be foolish not to accept the scholarship.

From then on, when people asked what I was going to do after graduation, I bragged, "I'm going to college in North Carolina." Most of the Home's graduating seniors—at least the ones I knew—could only shrug their shoulders and mumble "I don't know" when asked that question.

Being able to say I was going to college was a real ego booster. But suddenly the talking was over and I was faced with growing up. In a few short months I'd truly be on my own, with no one to lean on. Despite my tough exterior, that thought scared me.

Looking for encouragement, I returned to reading Booker T. Washington's *Up from Slavery*. One of the statements I saw there was, "The Negro youth starts out with the presumption against him."

I felt I could relate, at least somewhat. I'd been isolated, not because of my color, but because of my social and economic status. I was entering an adult world where many people looked down on guys like me. What would happen if the other college students found out I was a kid from an orphanage?

Maybe my stock portfolio would give me an advantage. I hoped so; it was obvious I lacked some of the social skills most kids learn in family living. It helped to remember that Booker T. had been raised in a cabin with no indoor toilet or bath, sleeping on a dirt floor. He hadn't known much about social graces either when he entered Hampton Normal and Agricultural Institute, now Hampton University.

Like Booker, I was struggling to rise above my childhood. He won—and I wanted to follow his lead.

I also discovered that one of Booker T.'s spiritual disciplines was to read two chapters of the Bible each day, along with one chapter from Proverbs. He'd found Proverbs to be especially useful in his roles as a man, businessman, husband, and father. Since he was smarter than I was, I figured I'd stick with his plan.

As I searched for direction about the future, another piece of advice came from an unexpected source.

It happened on a beautiful spring afternoon, shortly before graduation. I was working silently in the yard with Tony Martin, the Home's gardener and handyman. He never talked much. One of the few things I knew about him was that he'd quit school after third grade to help his family during the Great Depression.

That afternoon, Tony suddenly stopped raking. Sweat dripped from his leathery brow. Turning, he looked me straight in the eye.

"Robby, I want to tell you something."

I stared. In my 14 years at the Home, Tony had never stopped just to talk to me.

"I've been here a long time, Robby, and I've seen hundreds of kids come and go. You're the first kid I've ever seen who has the potential to become a doctor, lawyer, or professional something. All I want to ask you is—when you get there, don't forget the people like me."

My eyes grew wider—not just because gruff, old Tony had talked to me, but because no one had ever talked to me in quite that way.

Meaning every word, I said, "Tony, I will remember this moment. And I will honestly try to never forget you or the people in your situation."

"Don't forget the people like me," he repeated. Then he turned and began to rake wordlessly.

I understood what he meant. It was his way of saying that everybody has value. It was his way of saying that people down the ladder of "importance" have feelings, hopes, dreams, and needs, too.

He saw potential in me when I hoped only to survive. And he reminded me to remember what it was like to be one of society's castaways.

I hear you, I thought. *I promise I will never forget what it means to be considered unimportant.*

Thinking that way showed something was slowly changing in my heart. But I still harbored a rebellious, antisocial attitude—and it was causing problems.

In an era when many American adults thought young men with beards were anti-war protestors, hippies, drug users, or social misfits, I grew a beard. The blond tones of my hair made the whiskers hardly apparent, but administrators at school and the Home came down hard on me.

As graduation approached, five of us seniors still had beards. Four of them, "Townies," began to draw serious heat from their parents and peers. A few days before graduation the four cornered me and said, "Mitchell, why don't we just shave? Let's all do it together."

"Guys," I said, "it doesn't matter to me what you do. But I'm not shaving. There's no good reason we have to."

They all shaved. I didn't.

When I walked down the aisle to receive my diploma, my head was held high. I felt a weird sense of satisfaction as disgusted parents shot me dirty looks.

In more than a hundred years, not one boy had graduated from Princeton High School wearing a beard. If someone had asked me why I chose to be the first, I probably would have said, "I really don't care what adults or my peers think. In a few weeks, none of these people will mean a thing to me or to my future."

The truth was that a war was going on inside me. In this particular battle, the angry and resentful old me had won. The new me was still struggling.

As the last summer of my childhood arrived, I headed back to church camp. Everything looked different somehow. I wasn't perfect, but I wasn't a "wild man," either. Those who'd known me the previous year were pleased to see the difference. Understanding that I was in the early stages of my new life, they cared enough to overlook my rough edges.

When summer ended, I went to Chicago for a couple of days to see Gigi. Neither of us knew where Mother was, which was fine by me.

When Gigi and I said good-bye, it wasn't very emotional. After all, I'd be calling her and visiting several times a year. As we hugged, she gave me a warning and a promise: "I still intend to live long enough to see you graduate from college and marry, Robby."

"I'm holding you to that, Gigi!" I said, and we both grinned.

Back in Princeton, my summer absence made it feel as if I'd already left the Home. The day before I was to leave, I said farewell to all the staff and many of the kids.

Last, but not least, was Nola.

Someone watched her current herd of Little Boys so we could take a long walk. Always caring but never sappy or melodramatic, Nola recalled me as the bouncing puppy I'd been when she'd first come to the Home. She remembered how the staff had struggled to keep me healthy emotionally, and how I'd cried nearly all night in second grade when I'd given up hope.

She'd hurt for me, she said, when I'd returned from being

abducted by my mother. Nola knew that had started me on a bitter journey made worse by my relatives in Atlanta who didn't seem to accept me.

"But, Robby," she said, "we never stopped praying for you. I never gave up hope that one day you would choose to come out of the darkness that was yours. I'm so glad I got to see you begin your spiritual journey."

As we laughed about other childhood memories, a thought struck me: *Is this the kind of talk that happens between a normal mother and her son?*

I wished I'd had times like those.

Suddenly Nola turned toward me. Instead of bending to her knees to look her "little Robby" in the eye, she reached up and took my face in her hands—as she always did when she wanted to make sure one of her boys was paying attention.

Her eyes were moist as she repeated what she'd told me so many times when I was one of her "little ones": "Don't ever forget this, Robby. God loves you and I love you, too."

The lump in my throat kept me from saying what I felt.

I wanted to say, "Thank you for loving me, for relentlessly praying for me, for believing in me and dozens of other little boys." All I could do was hold her tight and force out a husky "Thank you."

She kissed my cheek, wished me luck, and went back to the chaos of putting a dozen little boys to bed.

Before leaving town, I tried to apologize to the kids I'd wronged—the boys I'd wounded and the girls I'd treated in a less-than-gentlemanly way. I couldn't find them all. Soon I was packing my bags, getting ready to put Princeton behind me for good.

Gracious as usual, my cousin Art offered to drive me to North

Carolina that August of 1972. I loaded his car with all my worldly possessions—guitar, record player, record collection, two suitcases of clothes, a Bible, a bankbook, and a stock statement.

As we pulled out of Princeton, I didn't look back. I didn't wave good-bye. I just basked in the feeling of freedom.

I was finally out of the orphanage where I'd struggled for so many long years.

I was out of the town where some people cared for kids like us, but others treated us as second-class citizens.

I was on my own.

I didn't have a family or a home. But I had two questions:

Could I survive?

And could I ever become more than my childhood?

20

The Freshman

GUILFORD COLLEGE WAS A DIFFERENT world.

The Southern accents, the canopy of poplar and oak trees, the red brick buildings fashioned from local clay—everything about the 135-year-old campus reminded me that I wasn't in Princeton anymore.

That was fine with me. I was ready for change, eager to reinvent myself.

For starters, I buried Robby from the orphanage and became Rob. I vowed never again to let anyone turn me into a second-class citizen or judge me for something my parents had done. No more would I be looked down upon or shunned because everyone assumed a kid from an orphanage was a thief and troublemaker.

People wouldn't assume that about me because they wouldn't know my history. I decided never to open the book of my childhood until I'd found someone I could trust—a true friend who wouldn't run as soon as I shared the pages of my past.

I was determined to prove myself, too. In my first semester, I decided to try out for the basketball team.

After all, I figured, *I can probably be a hotshot in this small pond. A private college like this can't have too many scholarship players. I oughta be able to walk on and at least make the bench team.*

My goal had little to do with sports. It was to be accepted in my own right, not just tolerated. I hoped to show on the basketball court that I was just as good as the kids from "real" homes.

Little did I know what I was up against.

The first player I met at tryouts was M. L. Carr. He would go on to play professional basketball for years with the Boston Celtics.

Next was Lloyd Free, who later changed his name to World B. Free. He would become one of the National Basketball Association's top scorers.

"What are you good at?" the coach asked me.

"I'm quick," I said. "I'm pretty good at defense and ball handling, too."

"Okay, you guard this guy named Free." I think he smirked as he walked away.

I looked Free over. *I can handle him,* I thought. *All I want to do is make the bench team; I'm not expecting to make the starting squad.*

One of my high school coaches had taught me that when you guard a man, you should watch which way his hips move. "A basketball player can fake you with his feet, head, shoulders, or the ball," the coach explained, "but his hips don't lie."

Lloyd Free's hips lied.

After that first scrimmage, I felt like a shredded jock strap. I'd never been beaten so badly in my entire life. Humiliated, I walked off the court in a daze.

When I told my roommate what had happened, he roared with laughter. "Man, last year they almost won the national NAIA championship, and they'll probably win it this year!" They did.

I'll never know if I could have made the bench team. Maybe if I'd had a dad who said, "Son, you go back and give it another shot," I would have tried again. But there was no dad to encourage me, and no family to cheer me on.

You are just setting yourself up for failure! whispered a voice inside my head. Remembering my fruitless quest to be accepted on the high school squad, I quit. I didn't need defeat this soon into college.

Before long I was getting a closer look at how normal kids from real homes and families lived. That made the first semester tough in other ways, too.

When other guys got into trouble, were frustrated, or just felt down, they called home.

They got mail telling them which family members were doing what.

Their moms often called to check up on them, asking whether they were okay, whether they needed money, how their grades were, and if they'd met any cute girls. I envied them.

I called Gigi every Sunday afternoon, but didn't confide in her. I was sure she wouldn't understand my feelings, and didn't want to worry her. Once again I found myself in the emotional wasteland of loneliness.

As the semester wore on, I began to search for fellowship and understanding in Christian relationships. A few spiritually based discussion groups met on campus. But I was puzzled when I met many who considered themselves good members of their denomination without thinking of themselves as Christians.

Fortunately, I connected with some spiritually deep, retired men and women who helped me learn the old Quaker practice of sitting in silence and waiting for God to speak. But when I began to meditate, I wasn't sure how I'd react if I actually heard God talk. I'd probably decide I was on my way to a mental hospital like my father—or to the streets like my crazy mother.

The mentors I was learning from said the Bible promises that if we seek God, we will find Him. They explained that Christian meditation is a process of emptying oneself in order to be filled by God Himself.

It took a lot of work to slow my high-energy body and brain down so I could stop, listen, and wait on Him—even for a few minutes each day. But the practice not only calmed me, it helped me recognize that voice. Once I learned how to listen, God spoke—not out loud, and not daily. But occasionally, when I needed to be led, a phrase or thought that was clearly not my own would come into my mind, leaving no doubt about its source.

It was a form of communication God would soon use in a very unexpected way—a way that would change my life.

/21/

Home

SUMMER BREAK, 1973. MY FIRST year of college had worn me out. I was ready for a change of pace.

After flying to Chicago and seeing Gigi for a couple of days, I hopped on a bus and headed for Moline, Illinois—about three hours southwest of Chicago.

My friend Scott lived there. We'd met at summer camp three years before. Scott and his family graciously had invited me to Moline for many weekends during high school; now Scott and I would be working in Lake Geneva as camp lifeguards and swim instructors.

As the Trailways bus carried me along Interstate 80 toward Moline, I watched the fields flow by. In early June, the bright green stalks of corn weren't tall enough to hide the rich, dark earth beneath.

Suddenly a highway sign flashed by: PRINCETON 60 MILES.

I was startled. When I'd left town for college, I hadn't intended to return. Since I traveled by train most of the time, I hadn't realized that the bus would pass by the Swedish farming community where I'd grown up.

I could remember a joke we used to make about Princeton—that the town could afford only three stoplights, so it placed all of them on Main Street. I smiled, feeling more sophisticated than small-town now that I had a year of college under my belt. Surely my past was behind me, and I was ready to move on.

As we got closer to Princeton, I figured I'd merely wave a last mental good-bye from the safe distance of Interstate 80. But all at once the driver hit his turn signal, and we were diverted toward the little town.

Soon the bus was rumbling down Main Street. I gazed through the large, tinted windows as we headed toward the small hotel that served as Princeton's bus terminal. I, on the other hand, was headed for a crisis.

On the sidewalks were high school athletes who'd run cross-country and played basketball alongside me less than a year before. There was the Dairy Queen, where students who'd sat next to me in class now ate ice cream. I recognized guys who used to fling snowballs at me.

They couldn't see me behind the tinted windows of the bus. That explained why none of them waved or called my name or smiled or pointed. Or did it?

"Hey, it's me, guys!" I wanted to yell. "Look! I'm here!" They wouldn't have heard me, of course, since the window was locked to keep the conditioned air from escaping. But if they could have heard, would they have cared?

In more ways than one, I was invisible to them. Life in Princeton carried on as if I'd never lived there.

After pausing at the hotel, the bus turned and retraced its path. It stopped at the town's third and final stoplight before heading back toward the interstate.

With a slow-motion numbness I realized that the Covenant Children's Home was just four blocks east of me, down Elm Street. The kids and staff didn't know I was in town. But if they had, would it have made any difference?

Princeton was my home in name only. In reality, I had no home.

The realization hit me like a Midwestern twister. I usually had time to get down to some inner cellar before emotional storms from my childhood could blow me away. But this unexpected detour had caught me by surprise. There'd been no chance to barricade the doors.

I'd felt despised, ignored, and rejected before, but never invisible. Now it seemed that if I suddenly vanished, nobody would notice or care.

The guys running down the street or hanging out at the Dairy Queen were home. This was their town. Later they would retreat to the safety of their houses—places full of parents, siblings, and memories. But for me, the place where I'd spent 15 of my first 18 years was no longer home.

That chapter of my life had ended abruptly. The Home had no funds for post-graduation follow-up, counseling, or financial or emotional support. Nobody stayed in touch with us. No one phoned to ask if we were doing all right—or were even still alive.

It wasn't the staff's fault. Most of them worked hard for what must have seemed like 25 hours a day. There was no time for those of us who'd moved on. Struggling to make it on our own was just a stark reality, another dangerous set of rapids in the dark river of life we'd been tossed into.

I could remember how, when playing basketball at the Home, I'd tighten my muscles when I knew another player was about to slam me into a brick wall that held the goal. Now, as the bus pulled back onto the interstate, I realized I'd just been slammed—without being able to harden myself against the pain.

I hadn't been able to admit before that I couldn't go home. I'd danced around the subject at college; when other students asked where I was going during semester breaks, I gave vague answers and mentioned the names of cities I'd visit. They assumed I was going home. Explaining the chaotic truth seemed pointless, so I never tried.

Besides, I thought, *who can relate to my story?*

In the end, it just hurt too much to admit to my peers—and maybe to myself—that I didn't have what most of them took for granted.

Even the Home was no longer my home. That harsh realization was ripping me apart. Fearing the other bus riders would think I was crazy, I clamped my jaw tight and kept the storm inside.

Filled with fury, I hurled my thoughts at God. *Why couldn't You have given me a little place to live? I didn't want an Atlanta mansion. I would have been happy with four rooms, a little yard, and a dog. Nothing fancy. I just wanted a home with a mom and a dad. I didn't care whether we had any money. I just wanted a home!*

Why, God? Why this life? What did I do to deserve it?

I waited a few moments. Nothing.

Why don't You answer me? I screamed.

Silence.

Are You listening to me? I roared in silent rage.

Silence. Unresponsive silence, as if I'd been buried alive.

I stared out the window as the Illinois farmland flashed by. *I'll never be able to go home, will I?*

Despite Gigi's love, her apartment wasn't home. Neither was Atlanta, even though Uncle Arnold and Aunt Alice let me visit.

Wherever I went, I felt like a guest.

Home is where you can go without being a guest.

Emotional waves kept crashing over me like dangerous surf. After minutes of inner screaming, I was too exhausted to think.

Then, as the bus hummed down the interstate, a thought floated unexpectedly into my mind. Its entry was soft as a feather, and I almost missed it.

Call Me Father, Rob. Call Me home.

From deep within came my angry response.

You expect me to be satisfied with that? That doesn't explain things! No way does that kiss away the scars of the last 15 years, and it doesn't help now! Do You hear me?

I don't have a home. I won't ever sleep in my childhood bedroom. I won't be able to bring my wife to stay in the house I grew up in.

My children won't be able to play with their grandmother and grandfather. If I'm hurt, broke, or in trouble, I can't look to home for help!

Do You understand me? I don't have a home!

If God had a reply, my anger kept it from getting through. But I was too tired to keep up the defenses for long.

Finally I sensed the voice again. It was gentle but firm, like a loving command.

Call Me home, Rob. Just call Me home.

I sat in exhausted silence.

I'd asked to be changed, hadn't I? It had been happening—slowly.

And now, "Just as I Am," the God of the universe was offering to adopt me—*me.* No waiting period, no trial foster-home visits, no strings attached. I didn't even have to become a better person first.

He wanted to adopt me, a boy whose heart was covered with childhood dirt and wounds.

As the bus made its way down the dark highway, I responded.

Okay, God.

You've got a deal.

I will call You Father.

I will call You home.

/22/

Revelation

WHEN I RETURNED TO COLLEGE as a sophomore, it was with the confidence that God had offered me a spiritual home—a permanent one—and I'd accepted.

But I still had plenty of obstacles from my past to overcome.

For one thing, I was confused about how to handle the "sexual freedom" of the college campus. I'd never had a father around to give me a healthy view of sexuality, or a model of what love and marriage meant.

I'd been brought up with the double standard that said it was okay for men to sleep around, but not women. Now I saw that this attitude wasn't godly, fair, or smart. But I was meeting women who openly declared that if a guy was "hot" enough, they wanted to have a fling with him—and the interest some showed in me was a boost to my ego.

My old attitudes were changing, but slowly. I could recall how Swaney, my eighth grade counselor, had taught that sex was only for married people. But when opportunity knocked, it was tough to do the right thing.

One night my roommate was out of town. A girl I'd been dating ended up in my room with me. Lying on my bed, kissing, we were fully clothed but our bodies clearly were yelling, "Go!"

Suddenly an inner voice yelled: *No! This is not what God has called you to do!*

The clouds of steam in my testosterone-overloaded brain suddenly parted. Somehow I gathered enough willpower to swing my feet onto the floor and stand up. Both of us were surprised to hear me say, "We need to go for a walk."

As we strolled outside, she was clearly confused; I struggled for words. I wasn't sure why I'd stopped. Finally I cooled off enough to say, "You know, I really don't know what just happened. . . . But awhile ago I gave God a chance to change me, and all of a sudden I don't think this is what I should be doing."

For a long time that night, I lay awake trying to analyze the experience. *How in the world did I do that? Where am I going to find the strength to hold off the next time, and the next, until I finally get married?*

I'd seen too many kids like me become sexually involved, not out of love or even lust, but to fill an emotional emptiness. I knew it was time to remember that I'd changed and was still changing.

I want to be a man, a husband, and a father who can be trusted to be faithful.

I hoped I could live up to that standard, even without parental guidance.

I had learned, though, that if it gets too hot, stand up.

I could have used guidance when it came to declaring a major, too.

Constantly restless, I didn't have a clue about what career path to follow. I briefly considered becoming a research chemist, but a spring day when the dogwoods were in bloom convinced me that I couldn't spend the rest of my life in a lab. I liked studying languages, but couldn't see how it could help me make a living. Accounting looked like a possibility because working with numbers came easily to me, but it didn't really set off any bells in my head, either.

As Christmas break neared, I felt like a reindeer without a sleigh. I was wasting my time and the family scholarship. The only thing I knew with any certainty was that my future was in God's hands—and that if I let Him lead, I'd know what I should do.

One day a friend from Chicago mentioned on the phone that the church sponsoring the Home had a short-term missions program. Looking into it, I felt drawn to the chance to spend a year in Africa. The job: working as a "go-fer" for missionaries.

There was no pay, though. The church's outlook was, "If God is in this idea, He will provide. You are not to be a burden to the missionaries."

The program director told me I'd be expected to come up with $3,500 for my travel and expenses. I had that much in my stock portfolio, but dreamed of using it to buy a new car—a black convertible. After talking to those in the program and praying for direction, I sensed the convertible would have to wait.

Having prayed long and hard, I felt—with what young spiritual certainty I had—that this is what I was being called to.

Still, I hesitated when it was time to tell Gigi. I figured she'd be against my plan.

But when I called her, she didn't resist for a second. "If this is God's will, Robby," she said, "you go with my love and prayers."

My relatives in Atlanta didn't agree, thinking I was wasting my time and would never finish college. But by spring break, 1974, I'd made up my mind.

My professors at Guilford okayed my request to let me earn credits for my studies of French and the Congolese language of Lingala. I'd also get credits in African Studies based on my journals and a final term paper.

The thought of leaving the country for a year made me think hard about whether I'd see my older relatives again. It also pushed me to ask a question I'd never had the courage to ask before.

It happened at the end of the summer, after working at Uncle Arnold's car dealership and living with him and Aunt Annis. As the time to leave Atlanta approached, I said good-bye to Aunt Alice, Uncle Mack, and my cousins—but not Grandma Pauline, who was in a nursing home.

The night before my flight to Chicago, I sat for a final chat with Uncle Arnold and Aunt Annis. Arnold was now in his late 70s; I hated to think of losing him, but knew this might be my last chance to ask what I'd never asked anyone in Atlanta.

"Uncle Arnold, I need to ask you a tough question. I really would appreciate an honest answer, no matter what the truth may be."

He looked as if he knew what was coming—and had been preparing for years.

"I understand that Gigi was too poor to take me," I said. "Even if she wanted to, she wasn't strong enough emotionally or psychologically to fight my mother for custody. It would have been a constant battle with insanity. But I don't understand why no one in Atlanta would take me from the Children's Home and raise me. Why didn't any of you want me?"

I was surprised when tears came to my uncle's eyes. He struggled to compose himself.

"Robby, boy, I tried repeatedly to get Pauline to let me raise you. Your Grandfather Mitchell was not only my brother and a saint of a man, but he was my best friend. He would have wanted me to raise his grandson, and I would have loved doing that for him and for you."

I sat in stunned silence as Arnold paused, choking back his emotions. He took a gulp of bourbon before going on.

"The truth is your Grandmother Pauline refused to let me or any other family member raise you."

My mind raced, trying to understand. "Why?"

Silence.

"Why, Uncle Arnold?"

He shook his head, tears streaming down his wrinkled cheeks. "You were a social embarrassment to Pauline, Rob. Your being around Atlanta and not being raised by her son would have caused too many difficult explanations in her social circles. It was much more convenient for her to say you lived in Illinois."

A social embarrassment?

My own grandmother wouldn't allow other family members to raise me because that would have been too difficult to explain in her elite social circles?

I couldn't believe it. I was family enough to hang on to legally, but not good enough to raise. What a prize that made me!

So what does that make the family members who didn't have guts enough to stand up and do what was right? Apparently, not one of them even considered going against Pauline by giving Gigi money and legal help so she could raise me, either.

After the initial shock, I didn't know whether to feel outraged or resigned. On the one hand, this painful revelation seemed like just one more on a long list. On the other hand, I felt almost relieved. At least I didn't have to wonder any longer.

The next day I said good-bye. Aunt Annis hugged me and cried. Uncle Arnold discarded his customary handshake and, for the first time, embraced me. "Remember, boy," he said. "I have always loved you."

My mind churning, I flew to Chicago to see Gigi. After discussing my plans over my favorite pot roast, she said, "I'm happy for you, Robby. You do what God is telling you is right."

"I feel bad leaving you," I told her. "And being so far away in case you need me."

"Don't you think about that for one minute," she replied in her usual matter-of-fact way. "Besides, I hope I die while you're there. That way I won't be a burden to you. If you're in Africa, you won't know if I get sick and you'll be too far to come home for the funeral."

"Stop that right now," I protested. "You're not going to die while I'm gone, and you will never be a burden to me. Never!"

"Well, we won't talk about this any longer," she said. "But don't forget that you are to have the furniture and any money that might be left in my savings account."

Later, sitting on the couch just before bedtime, I slipped my hand over her frail fingers. "Gigi," I said, "I need to ask you a tough question."

"Go ahead, Robby," she replied. Her tone told me that she, too, had been waiting for this.

"Growing up, I never understood why my family in Atlanta

wouldn't raise me. It has haunted me for years. Before I left Atlanta, I asked Uncle Arnold why the family hadn't wanted me. Do you know what he told me, Gigi?"

"Yes, child. He told you Pauline wouldn't allow it. You were a social embarrassment to her."

"But, Gigi—if you knew this, why didn't you tell me?"

Her small shoulders began to tremble. I slipped an arm around her. "I'm not angry that you didn't tell me, Gigi. I just want to understand."

"I knew it when you were in junior high school," she said as tears began to flow. "But every time you asked me if you could live in Atlanta, it was too painful for me to say you never would. You had been through so much already I just couldn't be the one to tell you that you were being rejected again. Especially since the reason was so wicked."

Her voice dropped to a whisper. "I just couldn't do it. I'm so sorry—so very, very sorry."

She broke into sobs.

I held her as a father holds a daughter whose heart has been broken. I reassured her repeatedly that I wasn't angry, and was surprised to realize that—for the moment, at least—it was true.

I guess this is what the psychiatrist meant when he said I could intellectualize my emotions, I thought. *Put this in a box, close the lid, and bring it out at another point in time when you're ready to deal with it.*

Now was not the time for anger. It was time to comfort Gigi, who was crying because my childhood had been such a mess and there had been so little she could do about it. I wanted her to know that she'd given me what I needed most—the security that comes from consistent, unconditional love.

That night, it was hard to sleep.

The problem wasn't just the discovery I'd made about my past. It wasn't even fear of the African jungle.

The problem was uncertainty.

Tomorrow I was flying to an unfamiliar place to do unfamiliar things and leaving 80-year-old Gigi for a year.

But perhaps more importantly, I was doing something I'd never done—trusting that I'd heard God's call. And the idea of trusting anybody still made me very uncomfortable.

/23/

Into Africa

From Chicago I flew to Paris—then to Bangui, the capital city of the Central African Republic. My instructions: Wait in Bangui until a jungle plane flown by Missionary Aviation Fellowship arrived. It would take me to the city of Gemena, located in the northwest part of Zaire (Congo) known as the Ubangui.

Have I lost my mind? I asked as I stepped off the plane in Gemena. *It's hot, muggy, musty, dusty, and smelly here. I must be nuts!*

That first night, I continued to second-guess myself. *Have I come for the wrong reasons? Has God really led me? I'm turning 20 in a few months, and here I am like Tarzan on a comic-book adventure.*

After reflecting and praying about it, though, I felt more at peace. For some reason, God seemed to want me in Africa. And strange as the place looked to me, something exciting might be waiting there.

The Ubangui, a mixture of jungle and grasslands just north of the equator, grew bananas, oranges, lemons, limes, pineapples, mangoes, and papaya in abundance. To call the region remote would be an understatement; in 1974, the nearest telephone was 500 miles away and impossible to get to during the rainy season.

Missionaries served in seven locations, spread out over a 100-mile radius. Gemena, where I was stationed, contained the region's only post office and bank, the longest airstrip in the area, offices for customs and passport officials, a small army base, and a little hotel with a miniature, European-style restaurant right out of the movie *The African Queen.* A few small stores, a high school where our Protestant missionaries taught, and an elementary school with a Catholic staff completed the city.

Lee Anderson and his wife, Alene, my hosts and bosses, put me to work immediately. On September 10, 1974, I noted in my journal, "Have been working in Gemena nearly three weeks. It feels like months." I was grateful, though, to be learning so much from the Andersons.

The missionaries nicknamed me "Gemena Go-fer." One of my jobs was to "go fer" anything anyone needed.

A more crucial task was manning the shortwave radio—a vital link for the mission stations. Since the 1960 murder of missionary Paul Carlson during a violent Congo uprising, security had been a major concern.

Things had been tense but peaceful since Carlson's death; the memory still lingered among the missionaries. Each morning I flicked on the radio at 6:45 A.M. and called roll alphabetically by station. If everything was all right, a representative at each location responded, "Present." Three times each day the missionaries checked to make sure their fellow workers were alive.

Another assignment of mine involved tracking shipments of food, staples, and fuels. That was how I met Dapala.

In my first month of duty, we received word that a l[illegible] shipment was due at a river village named Akula, about 100 miles away. Dan, a short-termer, brought a flatbed truck filled with empty 55-gallon drums. We were joined by Dapala, a Christian from the major tribe known as Ngbaka.

Just seven years older than I, Dapala took care of the boys' dormitory and other maintenance projects at our high school in Gemena. Such a responsible job earned him considerable respect from his tribe.

As we drove, we used an assortment of cross-translations so we could understand each other. Dan and I spoke English; Dan and Dapala spoke Lingala; Dapala and I spoke French. Like the other tribesmen, Dapala called me "Row-bear," the French pronunciation of "Robert"—since "Rob" wasn't easy to pronounce in Lingala, Ngbaka, or French.

After bouncing down what they called a road—a dirt path with lots of ruts—we arrived safely in Akula and bought as many barrels of gasoline as they would sell us. On the way back to Gemena, though, the rains came and we had to stop driving on the dangerously slick jungle dirt roads. Fortunately, an African hunter had a shelter right where we stopped; he invited us inside to escape the downpour.

After an hour, the rain stopped as suddenly as it had begun. Out of nowhere a group of children appeared who wanted to see the white men. As I walked out of the hut, the mud felt enticingly squishy. Already sopping wet (and knowing I had a change of clean clothes in the truck), I couldn't resist the chance to play. Taking a hard run down a sloping section of the road, I slid baseball-style in the mud. The little Ngbaka kids went wild laughing, giggling, and clapping. *Kids are kids everywhere!* I thought with a grin.

Sensing the children's eagerness mixed with hesitancy, I reached out and grabbed one boy. Raising him in the air as his eyes bugged out, I ran back down the road, whooped, and held him while we slid through the mud. When we stopped, I said in Lingala, "Thank you."

He ran excitedly back to his friends, babbling in Ngbaka. I didn't understand what he said, but as I walked back to the group I noticed Dapala was grinning. Another brave boy cautiously stepped forward; I repeated the game with him, several other boys, and one girl brave enough to play with this white man.

When I'd slid with the last one, I asked Dapala to tell them, "Thank you; God loves you," in Nbgaka.

I was on my knees in front of this small group when Dapala translated my words. The little girl walked up, hugged me, then stared deep into my eyes. Her hands stroked my hair, traced the skin of my face, and gently twisted my beard. Probably for the first time in her life, she was close enough to inspect someone who didn't have black or brown skin; I couldn't imagine what this meant to her. She hugged me again, then ran back into the jungle waving good-bye.

When we pulled into Gemena late that night, Dapala made it clear that the experience had helped to establish a bond. He reached out to shake my hand and held the grasp for a long time. Smiling, he said, "You are a different kind of white man. I like the difference. We should be friends."

"Thank you," I said, returning his grin. "I will be honored to be your friend!"

Over the next month our friendship blossomed. Missionaries had warned me that considerable racism toward whites often surfaced in larger towns like Gemena, but Dapala's actions made that hard to believe.

Another incident, though, showed me the truth of what the missionaries had said. It also proved that the effects of my childhood had followed me all the way to Africa.

Next to my living quarters was a dormitory housing about 30 boys from local tribes. Occasionally we played soccer together. They often beat me with fancy footwork and dribbling, laughing loudly as they did, apparently enjoying the experience of outperforming a white opponent. That didn't bother me; I liked the challenge.

One afternoon, however, a player dribbled the ball straight at me—trying hard to make me look like a fool. He didn't find it so funny when I swiped the ball from him and passed it downfield.

A few soft snickers were heard, obviously aimed at the boy I'd embarrassed. After glaring angrily at me, he turned to his detractors and said something. I didn't understand anything except the final word—*mondeli.*

It was the Lingala word for white person. Missionaries had explained to me that the tone used when saying the word changed its meaning from a simple identification into a racial slur. I'd been told to be careful—to leave quietly if I heard the tone that indicated trouble.

There was no mistaking the tone the young man had used.

Suddenly, in what felt like super slow motion, I found my right fist closing, tensing. I heard the sound of flies buzzing. The "old me" rose like a lion who'd been lying camouflaged in the grass.

A familiar voice that only I could hear seemed to be laughing at me, coming from just inside the jungle that lined the soccer field. *Smash his face in! Hit, hit, hit, and he'll be down before he knows it and hurting for a week!*

You can't escape your past. Do it! Do it now!

But then there was another voice, calm and intense: *Don't hit him. Don't ruin the missionaries' work. Turn the other cheek and walk away.*

You have changed. Prove it to yourself and others!

Before the warring parts of me could decide, the Ngbaka boy who'd invited me to play jumped between my opponent and me, silently staring down this jungle schoolyard bully.

I raised my hand as a signal to be replaced, walked calmly to the sidelines, and excused myself a few minutes later.

Walking back to my hut, I thought about what had happened.

I wonder if this is what my missionary mentor was talking about when he tried to explain that judgment is getting what we deserve, mercy is not getting what we deserve, and grace is getting more than we deserve.

My old self had been ready to execute judgment. My slowly changing new self tried to persuade me to show mercy. Then grace had appeared in the form of the young Ngbaka tribesman who came to my aid. *Amazing!* I thought.

Mercy and grace, it seemed, were the only things that might help me escape the lion of my childhood anger.

There was still the problem of learning to trust, however. It turned out that Dapala would be my instructor in that subject.

That class began one day in December of 1974, after I'd been in Africa for four months. Dapala greeted me with his usual warm handshake, then made a request. "Row-bear, I've been asked to chaperone some teenage boys to a Big Sunday service. I need your help. Every three months, we African Christians from the Gemena area hold a special service at different villages deep in the jungle. Normally the head of the school drives, but he let me know he can't come. I can't drive a truck. Will you drive the truck for me?"

I hesitated. When Dapala said "deep in the jungle," I heard "near the end of the world." But getting to watch the tribespeople preach and sing was always appealing, so I agreed.

We made good time for the first 15 miles, the group of boys singing up a storm in the back of the truck. Soon Dapala pointed off the main dirt road onto one that wasn't much larger than a path. I turned; Dapala motioned for me to stop.

Out of the jungle stepped a tribesman. Apparently the local communication system—drums—had telegraphed that we were coming. Dapala jumped off the truck to chat with his friend.

When Dapala hopped back into the cab, he was carrying a large leaf his friend had given him. I'd just started the truck down the jungle path when Dapala said the leaf contained a favorite native dish and offered some to me.

The defenses of my old self instantly jumped up.

Are you nuts? I thought. *Except for Gigi and Nola, you can't trust anybody!*

This tribesman is trying to get you to eat something strange. You don't know what it is, if it's been properly cooked. Is it safe? Will it make you sick? There's no way you can ask him all these questions without insulting him.

Don't eat it! Don't trust him! It's not safe.

Then my changing, new self spoke up.

What's not safe? The food, or trusting?

My old self couldn't answer that question.

My new self decided to try trusting Dapala. Without looking, I reached into the leaf, grabbed some of the mysterious substance between my thumb and forefinger, and stuffed it into my mouth.

After chewing for a few moments, I guessed the munchy,

crunchy, nutty snack was palm nut fiber—mixed with fried army ants or termites.

I kept chewing slowly and carefully. No matter how long I chewed, though, I was constantly picking antennae and stray fibers out of my teeth.

A boy in the back of the truck kept watching through the rear window. Each time he reported that I'd taken another bite, the others howled with laughter. Dapala grinned broadly, clearly pleased at my willingness to share this delicacy.

The Big Sunday meeting drew dozens of tribespeople, including plenty of excited children. Dapala introduced me to several men and their wives. Within an hour of our arrival the sun had vanished, the jungle night wrapping the village in its deep shroud. Without the glow of small fires and a few flickering oil lanterns, I could not have seen my hand in front of my face.

After conversations and singing in Ngbaka, it was time for dinner. Before the food was served, Dapala asked loudly, "Row-bear, did you like what you ate on the road this afternoon?"

"But of course!" I replied. Then, frowning, I asked, "Dapala, friend, exactly what did I eat?"

"It was a termite," Dapala said, grinning. "The kind that builds huge dirt structures. It was fried in palm oil."

"They really weren't that bad," I said with a smile, "except their antennas and pincers kept getting stuck in my teeth."

The group laughed and clapped with glee. I could tell Dapala was pleased with me, perhaps even proud.

After dinner, we sang late into the night. Finally Dapala signaled that it was time to turn in.

As Dapala and I walked away from the fire, he reached over and loosely held my hand. If that had happened in the U.S., I might have been startled—but not here. A missionary had explained to me that it was a way of saying, "This man is closer than a brother. This is a man worth dying for."

I'd never seen a tribesman holding hands in public with a *mondeli.* I found out later that it was extremely rare.

As we walked, Dapala said quietly—not so much to engage me in conversation as to teach me—"Row-bear, these are my tribesmen, my villages, my family. I am nothing without them."

He led me to a large house with four rooms, a mud floor, mud walls, and a grass roof. We were to sleep in the same room, which held a large, bamboo-framed bed with a grass mat and a smaller bamboo bed. Dapala insisted I take the larger one.

My flashlight provided the only light as we sat on the edges of our beds. I asked what language he wanted to pray in before we went to sleep; he suggested each of us pray in his own tongue.

Reaching out to hold my hands, my friend prayed to the God of the universe in a language I didn't understand—except when he ended, "*Jesu Christe.*" I prayed in a language foreign to Dapala, except when I concluded with "Jesus Christ."

As we finished, I looked deeply into his dark eyes and said in Lingala, "We come from such different tribes . . . yet the same God understands and loves us."

After saying good night, I turned off the flashlight and lay in the pitch black of our jungle hut. I needed no light to see the truth: No matter where I was, God was there for me and for everyone—regardless of culture, language, history, or color.

A new identity was starting to emerge.

I am no longer just a kid from an orphanage, I thought. *I belong to God's global family.*

I still had many issues to work through. But on that night, a bit more of the scar tissue from my childhood fell away.

In June 1975 my time in Africa came to an end. Saying good-bye to my missionary hosts and Ngbaka friends was difficult.

On the day I left, Dapala and I exchanged no words—only a long, silent embrace. I shed tears of gratitude for his friendship. Sadly realizing I probably would never see him again in this life, I got into the truck and didn't look back.

Eight of us left the mission station that day. We spent several weeks driving 2,000 amazing, adventurous, and dangerous trans-African miles ending in Nairobi, Kenya—seeing everything from Pygmies in the Ituri forest, to machine-gun-toting men in Rwanda, to the game lands of the Serengeti, to the Ngorongor Crater. I would have plenty of stories to tell Gigi when I got home.

But the most important part of my mission trip had been a development in my own story. I'd gone to Africa as an uncertain boy from an orphanage. I was leaving with a greater willingness to trust—and a greater certainty that my adoption into God's world-wide family didn't depend on my culture or my past.

/24/

Forgive?

Before heading back to Guilford, I spent a week with Gigi at her apartment. Physically weaker but still mentally sharp, she'd turned 81 while I'd been gone. We spent wonderful hours together as I reported on my trip; every detail seemed important to her.

I also had a short debriefing session at the Covenant World Missions office. When the director handed me a refund from my expense account, I was astonished.

"You'd better check that account, sir," I protested. "That's more than what I had before I left."

"That's what you have left, Rob," he assured me. "While you were away, various groups and individuals contributed several thousand additional dollars to the $3,500 you started with. It's not unusual for our short-timers to end up with a refund. Many times we have seen God provide for those who answer the call on their lives. It's no surprise to us anymore."

When I left with my check, all I could think was, *Another form of grace. This trusting God stuff is really amazing!*

Soon it became clear that trust wasn't the only area in which the last year had changed me. My bragging, defiant manner seemed to be morphing into a quiet confidence.

Perhaps the best evidence of this change came on my way back to college, when I stopped in Atlanta to see Uncle Arnold. I knew he despised facial hair, and I still had a beard. In high school I would have kept it just to prove my independence; now such a confrontation felt unnecessary, so I shaved.

When the taxi dropped me off in Uncle Arnold's driveway, though, I was the surprised one. He was standing in the driveway to meet me, something he'd never done before. Without a word, tears shining in his eyes, he wrapped his arms around me for a long time—only the second time he'd hugged me.

Back at college, I decided to major in social services. Being a survivor made me want to help others make it, too.

Psychology became one of my favorite subjects. In those classes I learned that some mental illnesses and antisocial behavior could be traced to resentment over insults and injustices—real or imagined. My professors pointed out the importance of "coming to terms with one's past."

But they seemed to avoid the concept of forgiveness. In a way, so did I.

I knew I hadn't come to terms with my past. In fact, I wasn't interested in doing that.

But then I heard the story of Corrie ten Boom.

A Dutch Christian, Corrie and her sister Betsie, their father, and several friends had been arrested in 1944 for hiding Jews to save them from Hitler's gas chambers. Betsie and her father died in the

Ravensbruck concentration camp; Corrie survived and was now in the United States speaking of the experience.

She often told how, in a church where she was speaking, a man had approached her and extended his hand. Corrie recognized him as a former Nazi S.S. guard from Ravensbruck. He'd stood guard at the door when she and Betsie, pushed at gunpoint into the shower room, had been forced to strip naked in front of mocking German soldiers.

Now he was asking Corrie to forgive him.

Corrie told audiences that at that moment she felt nothing, not the slightest spark of warmth or charity. "Jesus," she prayed, "I cannot forgive him."

But God had called her to forgiveness, and she followed that calling.

At the end of her talk, Corrie gave her listeners a loving but bold challenge: "Who do you need to forgive?"

I knew the answer. It took no effort to come up with my short list.

"Remember the words in the prayer Jesus taught us," Corrie said. "God's answer to healing from the pain of injustice is to forgive those who have wronged us."

Corrie had been called to forgive a man who represented hurt, pain, and shame. I knew God wanted me to do the same.

But I didn't want to do it. Crawling through the jungle among poisonous snakes and army ants seemed more inviting.

As the days passed, like the tip of a thorn I couldn't seem to pull out of my foot, Corrie's question kept coming back to aggravate me: "Who do you need to forgive?"

I finally answered as I walked across the campus one day. *Okay! I know who. You want my list? My Grandmother Pauline, my father, my mother. There, that's who! I've answered Your question. Are You happy? Now leave me alone.*

I didn't know whether Corrie would have been pleased with my reply. I did know that I wasn't, and started to tell God why.

Come on! If the professionals at the Home didn't try and get us to forgive the adults who dumped their garbage on us—or worse, abused us—why should I bother to try to forgive anybody? They aren't asking me *to forgive* them*!*

What difference does it make? Pauline's dead, my father's brain-dead, and my mother might as well be. They won't even know if I do or don't forgive them!

Silence.

For weeks I continued to struggle. As my senior year at Guilford got further underway, the task of forgiving began to face stiff competition from my studies.

One morning during prayer time in that fall of 1976, I went at my protests again.

Is this really what I have to do to overcome my past and even have a chance to have a real, normal, dad-mom-and-kids family?

I don't think I'm capable of forgiving them! Just the attempt seems overwhelming. Are You sure I've got the brains and strength to even try to forgive any of these three? You aren't serious about this stuff, are You?

Then came one of those times when a thought that wasn't my own entered my mind. This time it was only one word.

Begin!

Was God just tired of my resistance? I didn't know. But I'd

learned that whenever God spoke, prayer time was over; it was time for me to think and reflect on the message.

Begin? Begin where?

I was clueless to the dangers of such a journey. And the only one who could take it was . . . me.

Pauline

As I reflected on the three who'd caused me the most pain, I decided Pauline would be the easiest to forgive.

She had died; I had shed no tears.

Now I tried to learn more about her. A discussion with her daughter, my Aunt Alice, didn't go far. Alice was kind, but didn't want to talk about the past. Whether it was due to a desire to "let sleeping dogs lie" or because it was personally difficult, I didn't gain any insights.

My psychology professors had taught me to try to understand people's motivations, so I replayed and analyzed my memories of Pauline. I thought about how she treated Aunt Alice, Uncle Mack, their children, and her household help. It began to dawn on me that she'd lived in a different world.

In Pauline's world, her goals apparently were so important that everyone around her was expected to play his or her role in their fulfillment. In that world, everything was wonderful—including

Pauline. It was almost as if she saw herself as a role model for all women.

Yet this symbol of gentle, Southern femininity constantly lashed out at people and ideas that made her uncomfortable. Often she would begin a rant against my mother, black people, or Jews with, "I only have the best of intentions when I say this."

My insights into this woman might have been accurate enough, but I couldn't get hold of answers to my important questions: *Why wouldn't she let someone in Atlanta raise me? How could she deny me a normal childhood? How could I possibly be an embarrassment to her?*

I was stuck. All my answers were too personal. When I was little, I figured life had been bad because I'd been bad. Even now it seemed there must have been something about me—something I'd said or hadn't said, done or hadn't done, been or hadn't been, looked like or hadn't looked like—that had offended Pauline.

Time after time I wrestled with: *What was it? What was the* it*?*

Time after time there was silence.

I kept struggling. I recalled how Pauline had called me her "dearest Robby" and told me she loved me. I remembered how, more than once, she'd said, "Oh, Robby, I'm so happy you are living in such a good place." I recalled how she sent $60 a month toward my bills at the Home, often reminding me of "all the expenses I pay."

In her mind, apparently, I lived in an idyllic setting—growing up in a comfortable cottage surrounded by happy playmates and attentive nannies. The Home may have beaten most of the alternatives, but it was no match for her fantasy.

Still, these ruminations did nothing to answer my biggest question: *What was it about me that turned her away?*

One morning, after hammering heaven with that question, I found myself thinking a thought that couldn't have been mine. It never would have occurred to me.

Nothing.

I was getting good at protesting. *What do You mean, "Nothing"? We're not talking about a poorly chosen word or a forgotten birthday card! We're talking about my entire childhood!*

Silence. Apparently God was going to make me figure this out on my own.

I remained stuck—until a college friend told me a story.

He'd gone out on Saturday night with a new girl he was goofy about. After taking her home, he was driving back to his parents' house in his dad's car. Thinking about the incredible good-night kiss his date had given him, he'd missed a curve and driven straight into a telephone pole.

Fortunately, he didn't get hurt. The car, on the other hand, needed intensive care.

"I felt really bad and stupid," he told me. "But Dad was furious. He wanted to smell my breath for booze and my shirt for marijuana. He even asked the cops to give me an alcohol test. It was embarrassing, even though I hadn't done any of those things. All night long Dad kept yelling, 'How could you do this to me?' "

"What did you say back?" I asked.

"For quite a while I said nothing. I love my dad, and know him pretty well. He just needed to vent. After church and at lunch he said it again, this time with less passion. I simply said, 'Dad, it wasn't personal. It had nothing to do with you. I was daydreaming and made a mistake, a bad mistake—but I didn't do it to hurt you. It was me being stupid and careless. It had nothing to do with you.' "

After my friend and I finished talking, I went for a long walk.

Sometimes you have a weird way of communicating, God. Really weird!

I knew God didn't cause the wreck to teach me a lesson, but I was learning something. Could it be that Pauline's actions had little to do with me? Was it possible that forcing me to grow up in an orphanage instead of with one of my rich great-uncles wasn't personal at all?

Maybe she didn't want Mother to visit—or, even worse, move to—Atlanta. Perhaps Pauline just avoided unpleasant things by pretending they didn't exist.

Could it be that she never dreamed she was being mean to me? After all, she assumed I lived in the wonderful fantasy world she'd created. On the other hand, maybe she was simply too self-absorbed to think about how I might be affected.

I knew there would always be lingering effects from Pauline. But she was dead now and couldn't directly hurt me. I had to remind myself that what she'd done in the past had nothing to do with who I was now.

If and when those inner voices tried to claim that my rejection by Pauline must have been personal, I could tell them that she was like my college buddy. Just as his accident wasn't an attack on his father, Pauline's actions weren't directed at me. I'd spent years wondering what I'd done wrong, and perhaps it wasn't about me at all.

There was no joy in this insight, but it was a step down the road of forgiveness. After wrestling with the issue for another couple of weeks, I came to the point where I could pray honestly and sincerely about it.

"God, Pauline hurt me. But I don't believe she meant to. I

believe she just meant to make her life easier. She was selfish, and in all of her selfishness she hurt many people, not just me. Even though she will never know it, I forgive her. If my anger toward her comes back, please help me to forgive her again."

God answered that prayer. He helped me let go of my anger toward Pauline, and threw it "as far as the east is from the west."

One down, two to go.

Forgiving Pauline had been tough. I was surprised to find it wasn't impossible.

Forgiving my father was going to be far more difficult.

/26/

Father

As I started the quest to understand my father, the first thing that came to mind was Gigi's story of the wedding furniture. It seemed to illustrate the battlefield on which my father must have struggled to survive.

A house may be a man's castle, but decorating it usually seems to be a wife's joy. Not in Pauline's world, apparently. From a distance of over a thousand miles she'd orchestrated what I'm sure she thought was a marvelous wedding gift. Without discussing it with her son or his new wife, she'd hired movers to remove and replace the furnishings in the newlyweds' apartment.

The replacements were expensive—brand-new mahogany. They were also complete—couch, chair, lamps, lamp stands, dining table, coffee table, chest of drawers, dresser, large mirror, desk, and king-size bed.

I tried to imagine my father's face as he opened the door and carried his bride over the threshold. Their furniture had vanished.

Their cozy new home had been turned into another woman's version of a proper Southern mansion.

It wasn't hard to picture Mother's rage. Years later, she still spit out the words every time she said, "Your father was a stupid weakling. He never once stood up to that conniving woman!"

I had little trouble recognizing my father's dilemma. He was caught between two strong-willed women.

Based on what Gigi and Mother had told me about him, Father hated confrontation. I figured he'd learned at an early age that bending to Pauline's will was the easiest path to follow. That left him with learning how to handle Mother's uncontrolled rages.

Perhaps he'd tried to calm Mother down by explaining that the furniture was more than he could afford and they'd be wise to keep it. She wouldn't have cared if the gift had cost a million dollars, of course. Her anger stemmed from "that woman's presumptive interference in our life."

So there he was, trapped between a ranting wife and a "helpful" mother. The two of them must have seemed like the tormenting harpies I'd read about in Dante's *Inferno*; my father couldn't find a way to free himself from their claws and constant pecking.

When I tried to discover something about Father's job in advertising, I reached a dead end. Gigi didn't know anybody who'd worked with him, and Aunt Alice didn't remember any of his former friends from Atlanta. But I knew advertising was a demanding, high-pressure field; he probably labored under daily stress.

My birth and Mother's mood swings must have ratcheted the pressure up a notch.

"More than once your frantic father called me after coming home to their apartment and finding you alone," Gigi told me. "You would be in your crib in soiled diapers, crying from hunger. Your mother was nowhere to be found and there was no note telling where she had gone.

"A few of those times, Joyce didn't even come home that night. When she did return, she never explained where she had been or even tried to justify leaving you alone. She just acted as if nothing was wrong and flew into a rage when your poor father questioned her. So he stopped. In a weird way, it seemed that each time your father didn't bother to confront her and demand an explanation, your mother seemed to respect him less. It was as if in her mind he had changed from her saving prince into a wimpy toad."

I was surprised at Gigi's candor. She softened her report by adding, "I always felt that poor Robert turned to alcohol to ease his stress. As things got worse at home and their marriage deteriorated, his drinking increased. I suppose the alcohol added another layer of conflict and difficulty to his life as he tried to hide it at work. But then your mother also was drinking heavily and taking some kind of goof pills. It was a terrible situation, Robby, and I couldn't do a thing to stop it."

I couldn't bring myself to call Father "poor," though I did feel sorry for him. Still, there must have been other choices he could have made.

Soon I faced a difficult question. How could my father leave his wife and son and go back to his manipulative, domineering mother? If he'd left Chicago and taken me with him, I might have understood.

But why would Father leave me with Mother when he knew she didn't take good care of me?

I couldn't find answers to those questions.

As for my father's suicide attempt, I'd learned some things about that subject while volunteering as a college student at a crisis telephone hotline. I'd been told that people who attempt suicide often talk about a stifling desperation. Some feel they're drowning in hopelessness, failure, and worthlessness. Many experience a suffocating sense of being unloved and unwanted.

This darkness can overwhelm the victim, pushing aside rationality and the drive for self-preservation. Most human beings scream for help when in trouble, but that cry doesn't always arise in the presuicidal mind and heart.

It was painful, trying to understand the darkness that must have surrounded my father. But I had to answer a question that had always haunted me: *How could you leave me?*

Eventually a dim light began to peek over the horizon.

Could it be that, like Pauline, my father's choices had nothing to do with me at all?

If my father could talk rationally now, what would he say? Maybe, I thought, it would go something like this: "Son, the clouds of hopelessness were closing over me. All I had left was the drive to survive, to protect my physical and emotional existence. The depression was so intense it overtook my reasoning and I simply couldn't think of anyone else."

Perhaps Father had left me emotionally long before he left Chicago. As his career and marriage collapsed, he probably felt like a failure. His gloom must have grown deeper at the prospect of having to admit these setbacks to his mother.

I could almost hear Pauline's response when he admitted his life was in shreds: "I only had the best intentions for you, Robert, when I suggested that perhaps you should not marry Joyce. If you had listened to me you wouldn't be in this situation now."

I didn't know for sure, but suspected my father never went for help. If he did, the counseling was not effective. I also didn't know why he chose the basement of Pauline's home for his final demonstration of pain. Maybe he was crying out, hoping someone would hear. Perhaps, consciously or not, he wanted to strike his mother in the place that would hurt her most, to embarrass her socially.

I didn't know why my father couldn't handle the pressures or put them in perspective. It seemed to me that he could have found a less stressful job and sought marriage counseling. He could have seen a doctor or counselor. He could have asked his sister, Alice, or his mother-in-law, Gigi, to raise me while he got help for himself and his wife.

Once again, I was stuck. I wanted to understand this man so that I could truly forgive him. I began to wonder: Would it help to go to the mental hospital and finally meet this stranger who had so affected my life?

During a visit to Atlanta, I talked it over with Uncle Arnold.

"Out of love for your Grandfather Mitchell," he said, "I go to visit your father every month. But you need to understand that if you visit him he won't know who you are. I've talked to the hospital doctors about your coming with me. They told me if he does understand who you are, he may have a violent reaction. Not because of you, but because you represent his failed life.

"Rob, you've told me you have no memory of your father. What will you gain from having as your one memory that of a man who can walk but can't dress himself, a man who can't talk in a complete sentence, a man who often has to wear diapers because he can't control his bladder? I'll do what you want, boy. I'll take you there if you insist, but why do you want this picture in your mind?"

I struggled with Uncle Arnold's counsel. Eventually, though, I agreed that having no mental picture of my father was better than having that one.

When I talked to God about the matter, it was with frustration. *So, You want me to forgive a man I do not know, do not understand, and have effectively never met? Can't I have some kind of understanding first?*

After several more days of wrestling, I reached the same conclusion I'd come to regarding Pauline: My father's choice to leave and to attempt suicide had nothing to do with me.

But, I told God, *even if I accept this understanding, it doesn't really help. A father is supposed to love his son. He's supposed to be a source of constant strength for his family. He's supposed to be a protector, defender, and role model. He should be the one who teaches his boys how to shave, to work hard, to understand women. How could he leave?*

I knew that millions of other people could say the same thing about their fathers. There was little comfort in that fact.

My inner battle took an unexpected turn one day as I was working with a group of young men and women who wanted to be lifeguards.

When everyone was treading water in the deep end of the pool, I explained, "If the victim won't stop thrashing, take a deep breath. Dive under the water, grasp each leg firmly with a hand. Twist the victim so his back is toward your face, then 'walk' up the body with your hands holding tight.

"This controls the victim and begins a sense of being held. When you have him under control you can surface, but don't release your strong grip. Place your right arm over the victim's right shoulder and across his chest, hooking your hand under his left armpit. This will instantly calm most panicked victims."

I demonstrated on a student, then let all of them do the same to me. "Now comes the tough stuff," I warned. "Not all victims will be passive, and I'm not going to be, either. You get one attempt before the next person tries, and then we'll repeat it."

As they tried to rescue me, I kicked, thrashed, climbed on their heads, and held them underwater. Afterward, the stunned and exhausted young men and women looked at me as though I were insane.

"You almost killed me!" gasped one.

"I thought I was supposed to save you!" challenged another.

"I thought I was going to die," complained a third.

I explained that this was how panicked victims acted. "They're not rational enough to realize you're trying to save them."

"But, Rob," a student protested, "we both could have drowned!"

That was my point, of course. "Never, ever, forget the rule," I said. "It's better that one person drowns rather than two." Then I added, "You can't save someone who won't let you save them."

Later, showering alone in the locker room, I realized how that reality applied to me.

Maybe my father had to let go of me while he tried to save himself. Perhaps he'd decided that if he couldn't save himself, he couldn't save me, either. Maybe he'd hoped the river of life would be kind to his little boy, washing me up on some peaceful shore.

I regretted my father's decisions, and that he appeared to be such a weakling. But I knew my pain couldn't change the past. If I wanted to move forward, I had to honestly forgive a man who didn't have the mental capacity to understand what that meant.

Standing under the hot water in that shower, I gratefully recalled the bus ride when the Creator of the universe had made it clear that He wanted to adopt me. Feeling as if I were standing under a healing rain, I quietly gave up my resentment toward my father. It seemed some of my childhood "dirt" was being washed away.

I took a deep breath, then exhaled a slow sigh of relief.

Two down, one to go.

Forgiving Mother would be the hardest task of all.

/27/

Mother

TRYING TO UNDERSTAND MOTHER WAS like descending into a Salvador Dali painting shrouded in a Kafkaesque nightmare.

At times it appeared possible to grasp her essence. Then another unpleasant memory appeared and that essence floated away, leaving me feeling I had to start at the beginning again.

How can I forgive the woman who symbolizes everything wrong with my childhood when she won't stand still long enough for me to get to know her?

As a little boy, I'd been confused about her behavior and how to act around her. As a young adult, I knew society and the Bible said I was supposed to respect my parents. *But how can I respect a mother who kidnapped me, kept me from Gigi, and then showed up stumbling drunk at my junior high graduation?*

I could remember one time when Mother had experienced a short period of stability. That summer Gigi and I went downtown to meet her for lunch. Slender and dressed in stylish clothes, Mother looked terrific. As we walked out of the building where she worked, men turned to look at her. A glimmer of pride and hope rose in my heart.

Unfortunately, that stability vanished like a snowman in a spring thaw. Mother wound up in yet another institution—and, later, on the street.

More sessions of electroshock therapy and numerous medications failed to improve her condition. When she was released, she abused alcohol and refused to take her medicines as prescribed.

When I reached adolescence, counselors at the Home had encouraged me to be sympathetic toward Mother, since mental illness was the cause of her actions. But after so many years of turmoil, it seemed too grueling to reach for sympathy.

Mother's decision to put me in the orphanage was a major stumbling block to forgiveness—especially since I'd learned that she had another option. Apparently a hospital chaplain had tried to get her to ask Gigi to care for me while Mother got on her feet. But Mother wouldn't hear of it, declaring Gigi a "high society" matron who wouldn't want to be bothered with me.

No matter how hard I tried, I couldn't understand what appeared to be such a cruel, spiteful choice.

When I saw Mother these days, it was reluctantly. She'd entered another halfway house the previous summer, close to the shadowy apartment building where we'd been apprehended a dozen years earlier. Occasionally I forced myself to visit her there—briefly—at Gigi's request.

At the halfway house the receptionist greeted visitors from behind bulletproof glass, admitting them only after they showed identification. Mother hated the procedure. "I'm over 50 years old and they treat me like a little kid," she grumbled. "The staff acts like they're caretakers at some zoo. It's obvious they don't think any of us will ever be well enough to live on our own. Their nitpicky rules drive me crazy."

Her room was barely large enough for a small single bed, dresser, and chair. The staff insisted she make her bed every morning before she could eat breakfast, then complete a list of daily chores. She earned points for everything she did in a system that rewarded her with extra spending money. I figured the place was good for her, at least providing shelter from the abuse she'd suffered on the streets.

For a couple of hours we'd sit in a nearby diner, sharing a meal. Since she counted out nickels, dimes, and quarters to pay the bill, I always ordered the minimum and only drank water.

Sometimes Mother sounded coherent, but in a second her talk could turn bizarre. She mentioned being homeless, hungry, beaten, robbed. I wondered if she ever prostituted herself to survive; she never said, and I never asked.

Occasionally she would twist her limited knowledge of the Bible into personal prophecies. One day she talked about my future wife: "I pray every day that you'll find the right woman, Robby. You make sure you bring her here and introduce her to me. Don't do anything foolish until I tell you she's good enough for you."

Yeah, right! I thought. *That's the last thing I'll ever do.*

One night, trying to understand her, I remembered the rainy season in Africa. Storm clouds there appeared to hover close to the ground; lightning was frequent and vicious. The ground under my hut would shake, making me want to run to a safer place.

I wondered whether Mother was always in the midst of such a

storm, mentally speaking. I never knew what her official diagnosis was. Paranoia? Schizophrenia? Manic-depression? All of these, or something else? Whatever the label, it was an unpredictable nightmare of depression, drunkenness, bitterness, anger, and disorientation.

I bounced between feeling sorry for her and being furious with her. One thing never changed, though: I didn't want her in my life! Just the thought of having to deal with her created stomach-twisting agony.

She's going to want to come to the wedding when I get married. How will I deal with that? How am I going to keep her from knowing about it? If she finds out she wasn't invited, there's no predicting what she'll do. Who knows what kind of comments she'll make to my wife if they ever meet?

I reminded myself, though, that Mother was practically penniless. Her only source of transportation to Greensboro would be hitchhiking—a challenge she couldn't handle at this stage of her life.

Still, the worries kept coming. *If I do marry, it will be just like her to come up with some stupid plan and announce, "Well, since I'm your mother, why don't I move in with you so you can take care of me?"*

If I really do forgive her, how will I deal with that issue?

And what about kids? Will I have to hide them from their mentally ill grandmother? Will they need to know she's unbalanced and lives in a halfway house? They shouldn't have to see her or be exposed to her!

It wasn't that Mother was evil; I knew she was just sick. At times I hurt for her, imprisoned as she was by problems from which she had no apparent hope of release. At other times I remembered the mountain of childhood pain she'd inflicted, and viewed her harshly.

I'd run into brick walls while trying to forgive Pauline and my father, but the attempt to understand Mother was much worse. I couldn't get through the chaos of Joyce Mitchell's heart, soul, and mind. The best I could do was to see her as a victim who sometimes struggled to rise above her mental darkness, only to be dragged back.

But was that enough? The fifth of the Ten Commandments, "Honor your father and your mother," kept bothering me. *How can I do that?* I'd protest. *How can I honor someone who has done nothing to deserve it?*

After countless hours of wrestling with such thoughts, I reached a difficult conclusion. In a sense, Joyce Mitchell had given up her right to be my mother.

She had given me life. But that didn't finish the job. Mothers were supposed to love and care for their children, and in my mind she had done neither.

I finally decided that all I could do to honor the woman who birthed me was to forgive her. It was time to stop holding on to resentment, time to move forward without judging whether she'd always been responsible for her actions.

But deciding to forgive and acting on that decision weren't the same thing. Logically, I knew forgiveness was a vital step toward my healing. Emotionally, I couldn't will my heart to respond no matter how hard I tried.

How, God? I prayed. *How can I forgive this person who has hurt me, embarrassed me, and abused me?*

The silence was familiar.

This battle came to a climax one Sunday afternoon. I'd developed an ulcer, and it had me swigging antacids straight from the bottle. The ulcer flared that day, just as the medicine bottle ran dry.

I walked to a pharmacy near the campus. Closed! Clutching my stomach, I shuffled back to my dorm.

My roommate was gone for the weekend. Sitting on the edge of the bed, bent over and feeling death would be welcome, I reached for my Bible. "Please help me," I prayed.

I flipped the Bible open. There I read, "Casting all your anxiety on Him, because He cares for you."

I'd seen these words before, but it seemed they'd been sent to fill the needs of this moment. Slowly I slid onto my knees and surrendered.

I give it up, God. I give it all up. The anxiety, the hurt, the pain. I can't forgive her yet, but I give You my anger toward Mother. Take it. Please! Just take it.

I knelt on the floor for what seemed like an eternity. Eventually I found the strength to get off my knees and sit on the side of the bed.

Less than an hour later, the ulcer pain had faded away; deep sleep arrived. When Monday morning dawned, I still was pain-free. Two weeks later it was clear that the ulcer was gone. So was much of the anxiety, hurt, and anger I'd harbored.

About three weeks after that Sunday, I asked myself, *Are you ready now, Rob? Are you ready to forgive your mother?*

Despite twinges of anxiety and a churning in my stomach, I realized God had shown there was nothing He couldn't handle. So I prayed aloud, "I don't want this to be a lie. I don't want to be fooling myself. I don't want to come and ask You to help me forgive my mother if I'm really not sincere."

I asked God to help me know whether I was ready by giving me a sense of peace about it. For the next week, a calm guarded my heart and mind. I knew the time had come.

At age 22, I got down on my knees and finally asked God to help me forgive my mother.

It had been three months since I'd started my quest to forgive

Pauline and my parents. The journey might not be over, but I knew my wounds could stop festering now. Eventually they would heal, even if scars remained.

Having chosen not to be a victim crippled by childhood trauma, I felt free—as if heavy chains had been removed from my legs. I was free to move wherever the river of life might take me.

I knew where I hoped that river would lead. I'd never given up my search for a real, human family.

That could only happen with the help of a wife who could see beyond my past—if I could find her.

/28/

The Lost Boys

NO CANDIDATES FOR THE OFFICE of Mrs. Rob Mitchell were on the horizon. That part of my search for family would have to wait. But as my senior year progressed, I would have a chance to find out whether I could relate to kids.

These weren't just any kids, though. They were castaways, too.

I'd already served as a youth group leader during my junior year at a church near the college. Now I signed up as a volunteer at the Nat Green Home for troubled boys outside of Greensboro, feeling I might be able to help. Soon I was invited to lead a combination Bible study and discussion group on Monday nights.

This Home contained a set of houseparents and eight soured-on-life adolescents. The "inmates" were just like the guys I'd grown up with; their issues were all too familiar.

It didn't take long before they challenged me.

"Who do you think you are?" spat a hardened 12-year-old as he stood toe-to-toe with me, glaring. "You can't possibly understand where we're coming from!"

Grabbing a fistful of his shirt, I picked him up off the floor with one hand and pressed him to the wall. As his feet dangled and his eyes bugged out, I said in a calm voice, "You don't have a clue where I come from. Now sit down and listen."

The boy stared as I plopped him into a chair. The other guys sat in silence, numbed by this handling of their self-appointed leader.

"Now that I have your undivided attention . . ." I said. "You have every reason to believe that no adult can understand your situation. You're probably right. Most of them can feel sorry for you, but they truly don't understand because they've never suffered what you have.

"Well, I do understand. I've been there. Abandoned at age three and stuffed in an orphanage, I spent the next fourteen years of my childhood there. At seventeen they gave me a one-way bus ticket to wherever. I've been on my own ever since."

Eight pairs of eyes grew wider. No one spoke.

"Trust me," I added. "I understand!"

After the initial shock passed, the group erupted with questions.

"Where did you live?"

"Illinois."

"You were only three?"

"Yup."

"What happened?"

"My father abandoned us, put a gun to his head, and pulled the trigger."

"Mine was killed in a drug fight! Your pa kill himself?"

"No, but he messed up his brain. He'll be in a mental hospital until he dies."

"Mine's in prison for another ten years. I see him sometimes. He don't care. You ever see your daddy?"

"No, I don't see him. He wouldn't know who I am."

"What about you mama? Where she?"

"Bag lady, streets of Chicago, in and out of shelters and halfway houses."

"Mine's a drunk."

"You got a grandma what takes care of you?"

"Sort of. She's great, but poor and old. Lives in Chicago."

"My grandma take care of me, 'cept when I get in trouble. Then she send me away to places like this. This is better than most places I been. You got brothers and sisters?"

"No, just me."

"My brother's dead. Sisters all married with kids."

While no one revealed the full dimensions of his story, all wanted to know the details of mine. I answered each without pressing for information. I knew it would be awhile before they trusted me.

Within a couple of weeks they loosened up, recognizing I was one of them. We talked about my feelings at their age and how I dealt with loneliness, rage, and personal problems. They seemed desperate for advice.

I'd always avoided talking about my childhood with "normal" people; it made me seem odd. But in this place, it was okay.

For these boys, seeing someone who'd spent 14 years in the "system" but had gotten out alive, wasn't in prison, and had almost finished college seemed to offer hope that maybe they could do the same. I began to think that telling my story might help others who felt abandoned, unloved, lonely, rejected, angry, or abnormal. During my year as a volunteer, several boys made commitments of faith and pledged to turn their lives in a positive direction.

Before I knew it, a milestone of my own was approaching. It was an event I'd once doubted could ever occur.

I was about to graduate from college.

I could remember thinking I'd never even be able to enroll. Many adults at the Children's Home had told me that as far as they knew, only two other kids from the orphanage had graduated from college in 20 years—maybe longer.

As far as I was concerned, my diploma wouldn't be just for me. It was for Gigi, who'd always believed in me, and for the boys and girls at the Home who needed to see that earning a degree was possible for kids like us.

Graduation arrived on a beautiful spring day in 1977. As I sat in my seat, holding my diploma, waves of emotion washed over me. I couldn't hold back the quiet tears.

I wasn't crying for myself. I wept for all the castaway kids who hadn't made it this far—and for those who still had a chance.

God, I prayed, *help me be an encourager to others who struggle with their own wounded pasts.*

I didn't know how that might happen. In fact, I had no idea what the future held. I was interested in seminary, but hadn't saved enough money. I did hope, though, to take a trip across the country—a sort of American safari.

To earn money for that journey, I found a job in a paper factory. I rented an inexpensive room from a widow who lived at the edge of town. The factory was a 30-mile round trip from my new place; in good weather I rode my bicycle to save money on gasoline. My co-workers thought I was nuts.

It felt good, becoming more than my childhood. Still, I wondered whether I might be doing too many things—working with the church youth group as well as the boys at the Nat Green Home—to prove to myself and the world that I was no longer just a kid from an orphanage.

Little did I know that I was about to meet someone who might be able to help me find what I'd always wanted—if I didn't blow it.

/29/

Seeking Susan

A FEW MONTHS AFTER GRADUATION, my friend David invited me to return to campus to visit the Bible study group I'd led the last two years. A rare October snow almost kept me from going, but at the last minute I went.

At another college across town, David's girlfriend, Annette, convinced two friends to go to Guilford to play in the snow with David and some of his football buddies. When the girls showed up unannounced at his room, David said, "Great! But after Bible study." The three girls, who were Christians, decided to attend.

As soon as I arrived at the meeting, my 23-year-old jaw dropped. I nearly stopped breathing.

There stood the most beautiful female I'd ever seen. This creature's brilliant blonde hair cascaded nearly to her waist, highlighting a figure that would have made any woman jealous. My heart raced; I was smitten, consumed.

It was tough to keep my thoughts focused on Bible study for the next hour.

God, please help me, the "new" me prayed. *If I can connect with her, let her be unattached. Help me make a good first impression, and help me keep my thoughts pure like You would have them.*

The "old" me just kept thinking, *Aroooooooooh! This hound is gonna hunt!*

After the Bible study was closed in prayer, I greeted many former classmates. Then I worked my way over to Annette and her friends, hugged Annette and met a girl named Phyllis—and turned to face the beautiful blonde.

The chaos inside me engulfed all rational thought. I was unsure of what might come out of my mouth.

She offered a gentle Southern lady's handshake and said, "Hi, I'm Susan."

When I finally realized she was gracefully trying to pull her hand from my grasp, it was clear that I'd held on too long. My opening line was brilliant: "So, you girls go to college with Annette?"

Susan gave me a quizzical look, but answered, "Yes, Annette and I are both majoring in interior design."

"Forgive me, but what is that?"

I cringed at my own question. *Shut up! Quit talking!*

"Space planning for residential and commercial spaces," she replied.

Get with it, dummy, I warned myself. *She's answering in short sentences. Get your act together.*

Susan reversed the interrogation. "So, Rob, what's your major?"

"I graduated in the spring and plan on going into the ministry." I just knew that would impress her.

"Oh, which church denomination?"

The right answer escaped me at the moment, so I finally said, "Christian." So much for impressing.

"Well, nice to meet you," Susan said politely. "We've got to go." She turned and left with Annette and Phyllis, who were rolling their eyes.

I wanted to chase her, but didn't move. I wanted to yell, "Wait for me!" but didn't speak.

Snickering, David waved good-bye as he followed them out. I didn't dare tag along; Susan's body language had seemed to say that my interest wasn't returned.

Still, she didn't know who she was dealing with.

There was something special about this one. It wasn't just her stunning beauty. I wasn't sure if my determination was born of ego, lust, or a deeper motive. But I began to plan my next step.

Since Susan and Annette lived on the same hall, I begged David for the number of the pay phone nearest to Susan's dorm room. I also begged him not to tell Susan he'd given me her number; I wanted a chance to invite her out before she wrote me off completely.

I called Susan's dorm repeatedly for three weeks. Fearing she would turn me down if she knew who was calling, I never left my name.

Finally I connected one evening. When I heard her voice I could hardly speak. At last I said, "Susan, this is Rob, David's friend. We met several weeks ago at a Bible study."

"Yes, I remember," she said politely, but without enthusiasm.

"I'm sure I didn't come across too well that night," I said, reciting what I'd already practiced. "But I really would appreciate a low-key chance to spend a little time with you so we can get to know each other. Could we perhaps see a movie or something at your convenience in the next week or two?"

Fully prepared for a turndown, I held my breath.

"As long as it is low-key, that will be fine."

Yes! I exulted. Then I gave myself a warning. *Calm down. Control yourself. Be brief. Don't babble like an idiot and ruin this chance.*

"Great!" I said with a tenth of the intensity I was feeling. After figuring out a day that would work, we hung up. Stunned, I leaned back in wonder. My legs felt like rubber.

Picking Susan up on the night of our first date, I saw a look of apprehension cross her face when she caught a glimpse of my car.

A few months earlier I'd paid $300 for my first vehicle, a Ford Fairlane station wagon from the 1960s. This rusting hulk's only redeeming qualities were a working engine and transmission. I'd had to remove the door panel and insert a two-by-four to hold up the glass in the passenger window. The floor was so corroded in spots you could see the road beneath your feet; a piece of plywood kept me from falling through. The vinyl seats were worn slick. Since seat belts weren't mandatory, it didn't have any.

Responding to a "Name the Bomb" contest, the kids in my youth group had dubbed this piece of junk "Wonder Wagon." They said it was a wonder the thing still ran.

Susan's reaction to the car was no wonder, though. It wasn't that she had expensive tastes; her father was a Methodist minister. But my relic on wheels didn't look at all safe.

After I opened the door to let her in, she took what might be called the "defensive date position." Sitting on the slippery bench seat, she turned her back to the passenger door and faced me instead of the windshield.

Driving along, I asked, "Are we on the right street to get to the theater?"

"You missed the turn a few blocks back."

"I thought so."

Hey, there's no traffic now. Why not take a U-turn? Without warning, I slowed and cut the wheel sharply to the left.

Immediately Susan slid across the seat, slammed into the passenger door, and landed with her rear on the floor and her legs in the air.

It wasn't very graceful.

She was horrified. So was I.

Feeling like I belonged in the Little Boys dorm again, I pulled the car to the curb, helped her up, and apologized profusely. Sweat popped from my brow and armpits as I waited for her to say, "Don't ever call me again."

Instead I got, "Don't worry about it, Rob. Let's just get to the show."

We enjoyed the movie, but afterward I immediately drove her back to her dorm. I wasn't about to risk making any more stupid moves. I didn't try to kiss her good night, either.

Unbelievably, she agreed to a second date. It went much more smoothly. We went to my room and talked for a long time; then I pulled out my guitar and we sang.

As I walked her to my car, she stopped to notice how beautiful the stars shone in the country. Impulsively I turned her toward me, wrapped my arms around her, and held her tenderly.

"You know, you fit perfectly between my shoulders," I said.

It sounded like a line, but we truly did seem to fit. After a brief kiss, I took her home.

This had the earmarks of a promising relationship, I thought.

But I soon discovered that my past would complicate things considerably.

On the afternoon of the day we'd scheduled our third date, I came home from work with a plan to take a shower and change my clothes. As soon as the front door closed behind me, my landlady hurried from the kitchen.

"Wait a minute, Rob. I need to talk to you about something."

Starting up the stairs, I called over my shoulder, "I'm sorry. I'm late for my date with Susan. Can we talk tomorrow?"

"No, Rob," she said firmly. "We can't."

That stopped me short.

"I don't know how to break this to you, Rob, but . . ." Her eyes lowered as her voice trailed off. "Rob, I received a phone call this morning. I'm so sorry. Your mother died."

I hesitated. When I finally spoke, it was with a lack of emotion I knew this lady wouldn't understand.

"There is . . . much about my childhood you don't know," I said carefully. "I was raised in an orphanage, not by my parents. It's a very complicated story. I promise I'll tell you more tomorrow. Until then, please don't think of me as a monster for not feeling too sad that my mother died. She wasn't much of a mother."

My landlady obviously was stunned by my response. Apparently realizing I must have reasons for feeling this way, she nodded, turned, and walked back into the kitchen.

After changing clothes, I left to pick up Susan. We went to a concert; as we sat together, I couldn't bring myself to tell her of my mother's death.

I knew Susan was a wonderfully sensitive person. But I still didn't feel free to share such news.

How can I explain that my mother's death is no big deal? I thought. *How can I possibly tell Susan that, in fact, it's a relief?*

I knew Susan loved her family. I also knew that if any of her family members had just died, she wouldn't be sitting at a concert. She'd be in tears, heading home to grieve. How could I explain my seemingly cold response unless I told her everything?

I wasn't ready to take a chance on what might happen if I did. So I said nothing.

After the concert I apologized for being so quiet. I asked Susan if we could end the evening early.

"Please believe me," I assured her, "this has nothing to do with you or our relationship. I'm just in a lousy mood and don't want to make you miserable. I'll call you tomorrow."

She looked puzzled, but agreed. When I got home, I had time to think.

Joyce Mitchell is gone. In truth, I felt relieved.

Since forgiving her, I'd seen her twice. Unfortunately, she hadn't been rational enough for me to tell her she'd been forgiven.

I wasn't happy that she was gone, but I wasn't sad either. At last she'd escaped the misery she'd lived with for 54 years. It wasn't my place to guess how God would judge a person who was mentally ill, but I hoped her soul was finally at peace.

Next morning I talked with Gigi on the phone. When I asked if I should fly back to Chicago, she said, "No, Robby. The shelter folk have planned a memorial service and Joyce will be buried in the pauper's cemetery. I don't feel well enough to attend, and all of her old friends lost touch with her long ago. I'm going to stay here and pray during the time of the service. That's all I can do for my poor daughter now."

I was grateful that Gigi allowed me to face Mother's death without having to fly to Chicago and falsify emotions I didn't feel.

But even several days later, I had no idea how to discuss this with Susan.

I was also beginning to realize a more disturbing truth: Thanks to my past, I had no idea how to have a serious, adult relationship with any woman.

/30/

The Relationship

Susan and I alternated between hot and cold. We'd draw close and hopes would soar; then one or both of us would get uncomfortable and pull back. These separations never lasted more than two or three weeks. Eventually one of us would call the other and we'd resume dating.

I had no adults to guide me in these unfamiliar waters. All I could think of were couples from old TV shows like *Ozzie & Harriet*, *Father Knows Best*, and *Leave It to Beaver*. These spouses were portrayed as perfect, finding solutions to all their problems in a half hour. They'd already done the hard job of courting, marrying, and having babies.

I wanted to end up with a family like theirs. I just didn't know how to get there.

That was obvious when I told Susan one day, "I'm not really sure where I'll be after I finish the American safari I plan to take this summer."

Her reply startled me. "I don't know whether to bother to try to keep this relationship going or end it. As a couple we have more potential than you're willing to admit. But I'm not sure I want to wait around for you to make up your mind about us."

Not sure how to respond, I changed the subject. I couldn't seem to explain that I certainly didn't want things to end, but was afraid to commit to more.

Somehow Susan put up with me long enough to invite me to China Grove, North Carolina, to visit her family. Beards were still a symbol of rebellion, especially in the South; the one I'd recently grown, plus my unwillingness to talk about family, put two strikes against me as I walked in to meet Susan's parents.

Her mother had cooked a delicious pot roast with mashed potatoes, homemade gravy, vegetables, and rolls. For a guy whose specialties were spreading peanut butter and jelly and boiling hot dogs, this was a feast.

Noticing that Susan's two teenage brothers ate only one serving, I figured they must have eaten a lot of snacks that day. When I complimented Susan's mother on the meal, she smiled and said, "Help yourself to more if you'd like." So I did.

To my chagrin, I later learned from Susan that her family, living on a modest pastor's salary, expected a roast to last at least two meals. When I'd finished eating, there'd been barely enough left to fix a sandwich. That explained why, after the main course, I'd overheard Susan's mother whisper, "Don't get too serious about this boy, dear. You won't be able to afford to feed him."

It also explained why, as Susan's father and I talked about spiritual matters in the living room after dinner, I overheard one of the brothers tell his mother, "He seems pretty smart. But boy, he sure can eat!"

Still, I emerged from this introduction unscathed. When Susan and I returned to Greensboro, our relationship seemed to go a little more smoothly.

Maybe it was because she seemed to understand my need for freedom—even though I'd never told her about my past. She let me pursue my mini-dreams, but always gave me a reason to return. She was the reason; not only was she a beauty to be won, but her inner beauty made me want to be a better man.

She challenged me in other ways, too. She had a way of asking "refining" questions. When I decided to rebuild the engine of a used pickup truck I'd purchased, she said, "You're putting a lot of energy into this project. What are your goals?"

"Just to see if I can," I said. It sounded better than, "To prove to myself that I can do a 'normal, manly' thing." Questions like hers helped me slow down instead of dashing frantically through life, trying to prove myself.

Susan seemed to know how to civilize me, too. Yet she did it carefully, always letting me be a man.

About five months after we met, I decided it was time to see whether Susan could handle the details of my childhood. Her response would tell me whether we could go beyond casual dating.

I was petrified. Trusting someone with the truth about my past still felt risky; I'd been afraid to tell the parents of my church youth group members about my childhood lest they decide they didn't want me around their kids.

Finally one evening I said, "Susan, I need to tell you about my past. Would you mind if we strolled around the college golf course while I talk? I'll feel more comfortable if we do."

My heart still raced as we walked and I talked. Susan listened to my story without interruption.

When I finished, I added, "So, if you don't want to date me anymore, I'll understand."

We kept walking through a long silence. With each step my heart seemed to drop another inch toward my feet.

Finally Susan stopped and turned to me. "Why would you say that?" she asked, incredulous. "Why would you think I wouldn't want to date you just because you had a miserable childhood? I haven't lost respect for you because of what you've lived through. In fact, I'm impressed that you've become so much more than your childhood. Of *course* I want to continue seeing you."

My heart might have leaped—if telling my story hadn't left me too drained. "I'll try and answer any questions you have," I said, "but can we wait for another time? Getting up the courage to tell you this was tough. You don't know how much I appreciate your response, but I'd really prefer not to talk about it anymore today. Okay?"

Susan nodded. Silently she pulled me toward her and held me tight.

I couldn't believe what was happening. I'd imagined a rejection scenario, not this one. *Can this be true?* I thought. *Have I really found a good woman who can accept me in spite of my parents' mental illnesses and my strange childhood?*

Over the next couple of weeks I distanced myself a little, building walls in case she reconsidered. I had to admit that if she did, it would hurt me more than I'd thought possible. I saw now that I'd never cared for any other woman as much as I did for Susan.

When our relationship didn't falter, I was stunned, grateful, overwhelmed—and scared.

I'd longed for a close relationship with a woman. Now that it looked like I'd found one, I struggled with more than one kind of fear.

How much can I reveal without appearing to be a monster?

How much can I share and try to work through with her before I seem too weird?

If this is the woman God wants me to marry, am I prepared to take that step into a lifetime commitment?

Still, it was exciting to finally have a girlfriend who seemed to love me in spite of my past. Maybe Susan really was the person who could get me to the "dad-mom-kids" life I'd wanted for so long.

Our relationship looked like an adventure in the making. With eager anticipation and caution born of experience, I prayed for the wisdom and courage I needed to be the man with whom Susan would want to spend her life.

I would soon learn I didn't fit that description as closely as I'd hoped.

The Swedish Covenant Children's Home in Princeton, Illinois, as it appeared during the author's stay. The main building contained dormitory units, staff offices, dining hall, and visitor's lounge.

Above: Joyce Mitchell, the author's mother, gets a hug from two-year-old Robby. The author's father, Robert, is at right. This photo was taken in April 1957, six months before Robert's suicide attempt.

Right: Grandma Gigi with two-and-a-half-year-old Robby

In the dining room at the Home, Robby sits at foreground right.

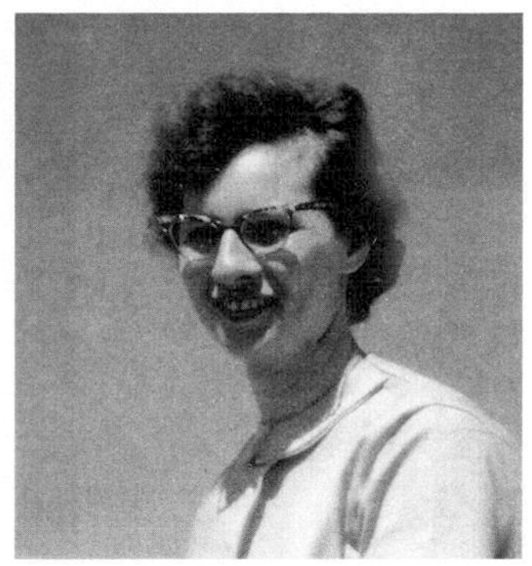

Nola, houseparent in the Little Boys dormitory, arrives a year after Robby did.

Twelve residents of the Little Boys dorm gather for a snack. The author, age four, sits at the far left.

Top: Grandma Pauline, 1955

Bottom: Joyce Mitchell, the author's mother, in 1967. She recently had been released from a state mental hospital, and struggled to survive in a halfway house.

Top: The author happily graduates from Guilford College in 1977.

Bottom: Susan Davis in 1975. "There stood the most beautiful female I'd ever seen," Rob would write.

Left: Rob's controversial beard was part of his look in 1978, during this phase of his sometimes rocky dating relationship with Susan.

Below: The summer of that year saw the author backpacking in the Grand Canyon, a highlight of his "American Safari." His grand tour of the U.S. didn't impress Susan, who was left behind.

Rob and Susan were married March 9, 1980, with Susan's father, Joe, (center) performing the ceremony. The author finally was beginning to realize his dream of having a "real" family.

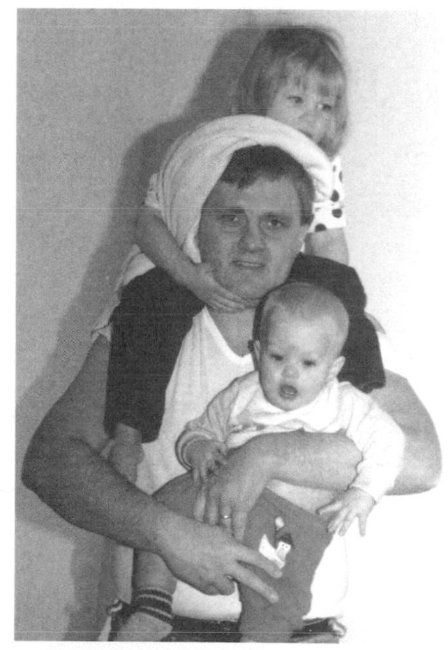

Kids were the next step. In this 1988 photo, Alicia, age two and a half, and Luke, age one, find climbing on Daddy a good way to bond.

The Mitchell family in 2002. Left to right: Luke, Rob, Alicia, Susan.

/31/

Separated

SPRING 1978 SAW ME TALKING constantly about my upcoming American safari. Time with Susan was often combined with adding a camper shell to my pickup truck. Saturday afternoon "dates" had me babbling with excitement as a relatively silent Susan handed me tools.

My plan was to spend 14 weeks on the road, with only one night in a motel. The rest of the time I'd be camping, sleeping in the truck, or staying with friends. I told Susan all about it—but paid no attention to her concerns until the evening before blastoff.

"I know you really want to do this, Rob," she said. "But can't you do it in shorter trips?"

"Not really," I answered. "This is the perfect time for me to go. I may never be as free from obligations again."

That didn't sound too sensitive, so I quickly added, "I'll be back, Susan. And I'll only be gone for a few months."

I tried to change the subject, but she persisted. "And what if you visit someplace on your trip and decide to stay there?"

That's a tough one, I thought. "Well, honey, I can't promise I will come back, but you're here—so that's a real good reason."

As soon as the words were out of my mouth, I knew how stupid they were. But it was too late. Susan's silence froze all communication.

I drove her back to her dorm, held her while she tried not to cry, kissed her, and told her I'd call when I could. She walked into the dorm without looking at me.

Why did you say that? I thought as I drove away. This stunningly beautiful, talented, intelligent, godly young woman wanted a future with me. Yet I was trying to keep my options open.

Why aren't you on your knees thanking God for sending her to you? Why are you holding back, thinking there might be someone even better out there?

I didn't have a clue.

That night my thoughts were racing so fast I couldn't get to sleep. Finally I shrugged them off, thinking, *Aw, she'll get over it.*

The following morning I jumped into my home on wheels and headed west. For the next 14 weeks I drove, backpacked, and saw America, from the Blue Ridge Mountains to the Olympic Peninsula in Washington State—and back again. In between I visited 84-year-old Gigi, saw Nola at the Children's Home, rode the Rogue River on a three-day whitewater trip, and took in natural wonders from the Grand Canyon to Oregon's Crater Lake.

Occasionally I found a pay phone and called Susan. When I reached her, she couldn't get a word in edgewise as I quickly summarized my adventures and told her I'd call again soon.

When I finally returned to North Carolina, there was Susan waiting in the driveway. Once again her beauty took my breath away. She listened for hours as I rattled on and on about the trip.

In my self-absorbed mind, our relationship was on track. We'd just go forward on our usual path.

I was wrong.

"I still don't know how you could leave me for over four months without promising me you'd be back and we'd go on together," she explained when I finally recognized something wasn't quite right.

Hey, I came back didn't I? I wanted to say it, but didn't.

"How did you know I'd be here waiting for you? You didn't ask me for a commitment. You just took me for granted and expected me to be here at your beck and call *if* you decided to return."

I knew I'd better keep my mouth shut.

"I'm glad you're back, Rob, and that you still feel attracted to me. But I wonder if I'm just a standby until something better comes along."

Why do women always have to get so emotional? I thought.

"Okay, honey, I get it," I said. "I should have been more sensitive to your concerns before I left. I was so wrapped up in the trip that I didn't realize you were questioning my feelings for you. I'm really sorry. Please don't write me off. Give me a chance to rebuild our relationship."

She didn't tell me to get lost. But I was on shaky ground and knew it.

The next day I found out that my former landlady had a room I could rent, so I moved back in. After working a few odd jobs, that fall of 1978 I took a sales position with a small company that marketed a new technology for electronic cash register systems. My bosses were helpful, honest, patient, and good teachers.

As my sales career developed, Susan was in the final stages of earning her degree in interior design. Soon the world would open up to her.

It was time for me to make a decision. I had to take the risk of asking Susan to marry me—or let her go.

But neither of us seemed ready to take that step. Susan confessed her struggle when she said one day, "I'm not sure you need me."

"I love you, Susan," I assured her. "But I'm not sure I'll ever reach the place where I need someone else to survive."

"But I need to be needed," she said simply.

How could I explain how frightening it was to even *think* of needing someone that way? Relying that much on another person would make me too vulnerable.

If there was anything my upbringing had taught me, it was to protect myself. It was a practice that had served me well at the orphanage, but it was starting to make my dream of family look like an impossible one.

/32/

Fear of Family

As if my fear of being vulnerable weren't enough to kill my relationship with Susan, I found myself haunted by the shadows of my parents.

How will I handle the situation if we marry and Susan displays the same kind of instability as Mother? I often asked myself. *Will I stay in the marriage or leave?*

If we have children before these problems develop, will I leave the kids or try to gain legal custody? Would it be fair to subject them to the kind of insanity I grew up with?

I knew many couples simply split if things went sour, giving their kids as much time and attention as was allowed. But the kind of marriage I wanted, the kind I'd always dreamed of, meant spending my life with a woman who was a partner—in money, in goals, in love and romance as well as spiritually. I never wanted my children to ask, "Why did Daddy leave?"

But what if Susan is hiding things from me like Mother must have from Father? What if I'm being ruled by my hormones and not seeing warning signs or thinking logically? What if she's okay now, but becomes crazy later?

I struggled for months over these "what ifs." Then, one morning during prayer time, I sat longer than usual with bowed head and closed eyes in silent anticipation of an answer. Just as I was about to give up, a thought I was totally unprepared for entered my mind.

What if you're *the problem?*

Bolting upright, I opened my eyes. Once again, we were at the heart of the matter.

What if it's me? Why haven't I considered that I might turn crazy like my parents did? Why am I focusing on her when I'm the one who's more likely to be the problem?

As usual, my eyes had been on how others might affect me. But what about Susan? How could I burden her with the possibility that I'd lose my mind?

If something like that happens, will I want Susan to leave me? If we have kids, will I be able to tell her to take our children away to save them from me?

It was the kind of question that had nagged me since childhood, the question I'd posed to John on the train ride back from seeing the psychiatrists in Chicago: "Am I doomed to be crazy like my parents?"

The question began to take other forms. *What if I'm not able to function in the world or can't hold a steady job due to mental or emotional problems?*

What if I come down with multiple sclerosis or another neurological disease that cripples me physically and makes me incapable of being a provider, protector, lover, and father?

Will I want Susan to abandon me because I've become weak?

The answer seemed obvious: Of course I wouldn't want her to

leave me. But for me to honestly face the reality that I could be the problem spouse took a lot longer.

It took a week or two of swallowing my pride before I could answer honestly from my heart. *No, of course not! I wouldn't want to be abandoned for any reason. I've been there, and it's not a place anyone should have to endure.*

Even if I do become the weak one, I want Susan to stick by me so we can face life's struggles together. I truly want her to honor her vow to stay beside me for better or worse, in sickness or health, whether we are rich or poor, for as long as we both live.

If I wanted that from my wife, how could I possibly demand less of myself?

After all, I wasn't the only one who'd be taking a leap of faith if we married. Susan's leap might be greater than mine.

I decided that the bottom-line question was, "Rob, are you ready to commit to this woman, to be faithful to her in all ways, no matter what?" I knew how I *should* answer, but to do it honestly and out loud was a major struggle.

Susan did her best to be understanding and patient as I talked with her to try and work through my struggles. One night I asked her to pray with me, and my request to God was direct: "Help me trust Susan not to abandon me. Give me the strength to commit to always being there for her as well."

For the week after praying that prayer, I was enveloped by a peace I couldn't explain. I finally felt ready to make that commitment.

We were lying in a hammock under Southern pines on a late summer evening when I asked Susan to marry me.

She never answered. She just kissed me so long and hard I thought I might suffocate.

When she started planning the wedding, I assumed that meant, "Yes."

A couple of weeks later, though, Susan still hadn't told anyone. "When are you going to tell your parents?" I finally asked.

She waved her left hand in front of my face.

"What does that mean?" I asked, irritated.

"My finger is naked!" she said with a grin.

"Huh?"

"I don't have an engagement ring, silly. I would like to have a ring first."

"Okay, take me to a store and show me a ring."

Apparently she'd already been looking. When we got to the store, she pointed out several in the showcase. Finally I asked the saleslady if I could hold one—so I could look at the price tag.

"Susan," I gasped. "There's a *comma* in the price! You aren't serious, are you?"

I didn't mean to embarrass or hurt her. I just hadn't paid $1,000 for anything in my life—even a car. But her mood changed instantly from verging on giddy to verging on sick.

"Please take me home," she whispered.

I knew enough to not say another word.

My poor landlady listened as I got this all off my chest. When I finished pacing the floor and expounding on the expense, I sat down and waited for advice. She couldn't look me in the eyes.

"What do you think you should do, Rob?" she asked gently.

"Do I have an option?" I asked.

She burst into laughter. When she finally could talk, she said, "No option at all, Rob. Bite the bullet, buy the rock. Welcome to the world of marriage."

I bought the ring and gave it to a surprised Susan, who cried and kissed me long and hard.

Soon we went to China Grove to announce our engagement to her parents. Her mom had already figured it out; her father hadn't. Once he recovered, he was very much in agreement.

One evening during our visit, Susan's dad asked me a question.

"Rob, as you look toward being a husband and hopefully a father, considering your childhood, who is your role model as a man?"

A list scrolled quickly through my mind: my older cousin Art; my high school social worker, Marv; Bob, the hunter; Swaney, the substitute houseparent; "white shirt" Dave; Lee, the missionary; Dapala, the Ngbaka tribesman. I couldn't help thinking of women who'd blessed my life, too: Gigi; Nola; Fran, Art's mom; Aunt Alice; missionary Alene.

Finally I answered my future father-in-law. "I don't want this to sound crazy, and please forgive me if it does. But I really think the best answer to your question is what I see in Jesus, the man. Obviously I could never copy His spiritual purity, but I would like to try to be like the man He was."

"Please, explain," Joe said.

"Well, from my studies, it seems that He was tender to little children, respectful of women, a friend to men, a defender of the weak, unbending under the pressure of great difficulties, fearless in the face of hypocritical and evil people, and faithful to God. He seems to be a pretty good role model."

After reflecting on my response, Joe encouraged me to condense it into simpler terms.

"A real man is both tough and tender," I replied.

Joe nodded.

"I want to be both—changing diapers and cuddling my children, but also doing things like weightlifting and hiking and hunting."

Sometime during the conversation, Susan had slipped into the room from the kitchen. She snickered.

"You know," I said, "you're going to have to be patient with me as a husband and a father. I'll need instruction. You're not going to be able to assume I know what to do!"

With a smile, a nod, and a twinkle in her eye, she assured me that this was no surprise. "Don't worry," she said. "I'm in need of a long-term project!"

/33/

Full Circle

In November 1979, Susan and I walked into the Chicago nursing home where Gigi was spending her final days.

In just a few months Susan and I were planning to marry. I was bringing my fiancée to meet my grandmother for the first time.

What would have been joyful a few years before was now bittersweet and difficult. Gigi, my beacon of strength, lay bedridden at age 86, too frail to get up to greet us. Fading in and out of awareness, she struggled mightily to sit up and talk.

St. Paul's House was clean, but carried an antiseptic odor mixed with the smell of decay. Susan and I had been led to this small sunroom where residents had been brought to face the outdoors.

There was some conversation among the elderly people, but not much. Most were sleeping, slumped in wheelchairs or propped in beige and gray recliners that sadly seemed to match their ashen skin.

Susan pulled up a chair beside Gigi's recliner, reached out, and took a withered hand in hers. Eyes that had seen so much pain searched my fiancée's face for the kind of details women want and men don't understand.

Gently smiling, Gigi squeezed Susan's hand. I stood by, the lump in my throat so large that talking was impossible and breathing difficult.

"For many years I've prayed that God would let me see Rob graduate from college and get married," Gigi whispered. "I'm so grateful I got to meet you."

She turned to a nurse who'd entered the room and proudly announced, "This is Rob's sweet little wife. They are going to get married in March."

We caught Gigi's confusion and smiled.

She shut her eyes for a bit, then opened them and asked, "Now, Susan, when are you getting married?"

"In March, Gigi. Rob and I are to marry in March."

Gigi didn't see the tear on Susan's cheek, but I did.

My future wife kept her voice light as she asked for a piece of advice. "How in the world am I ever going to feed this man?"

Gigi grinned, her wrinkles changing position. Her weakly whispered response was like that of a little girl sharing a secret with her new best friend. "He likes pot roast, mashed potatoes and gravy, spinach, and vanilla ice cream with chocolate syrup."

Susan nodded.

"I do need to warn you of something, though," Gigi added sternly.

Surprised, we both leaned forward.

"Dear, he's a sweet boy. But he snores like a chain saw!"

We roared. She still had her sense of humor.

Susan wiped her eyes, then started to ask another question. But Gigi had drifted back to sleep.

We waited a little while. Hoping that Gigi might wake up and talk with us a bit more, my bride-to-be took a bottle of lotion and smoothed some on my grandmother's arms. The paper-thin skin quickly soaked it up.

The eyes remained closed, but a smile took shape on the lips. "Thank you," Gigi said softly.

Soon we had to accept the fact that she was worn out and had fallen into a deep sleep. It was time to go.

Susan stood, then leaned over and kissed Gigi's forehead. I kissed her too, then held my head next to hers, hoping to catch a whiff of her favorite perfume. Sadly, she had none on. I wished I had brought a bottle.

Arm in arm, Susan and I walked out in silence. In reality she was holding me up. I still couldn't talk.

This wasn't the Gigi I remembered, the one I wanted Susan to know. I hadn't realized the state my grandmother was in; she had sounded stronger on the phone.

One of the reasons we'd flown to Chicago was so that she could get to know Susan. Somewhat short of that goal, we left with the foreboding awareness that my beloved grandmother's final day was drawing near.

We took a bus northwest to Rockford to conclude the other business that had brought us to Illinois.

When Art had moved Gigi into the nursing home, he'd stored what remained of the furniture Pauline had bestowed on my parents. Ironically, a bone of contention in my father's marriage now would provide comfort for his son's new family. We rented a truck in Rockford and loaded a small fortune in home furnishings.

Art also had saved Gigi's everyday place settings and some wedding gifts my parents had received—including crystal place settings, crystal glasses and goblets, and a beautiful set of antique silverware. Gigi's hope to provide me with an inheritance was fulfilled.

Susan and I transported her special gift back to North Carolina, where we began to set up an apartment.

Planning for our wedding shifted into high gear. My guest list was simple: Mitchell relatives from Atlanta and a few from North Carolina; my church youth group; a few college professors and friends. Aged relatives in Illinois would be unable to travel that far.

Susan's list was much longer. Both of her parents came from large extended families, and many people from her father's current and past congregations were included. Plowing through the lists looked confusing to me, but Susan seemed completely at ease.

Susan and her father often sat at the kitchen table, working out the details of the ceremony. They chose Bible verses, vows, and hymns. I knew I wanted to say "I do," but that about covered my opinions.

I was touched when some of my relatives stepped up to help. Aunt Alice and Uncle Mack hosted and paid for the rehearsal dinner at a local country club; Great-aunt Martha from Burlington hosted and paid for a wedding brunch.

Our wedding day in March 1980 was sunny.

The Methodist church in China Grove had beautiful, warm woods and stained glass windows. The bridesmaids wore maroon dresses, the groomsmen blue suits. Susan's dress was a soft white; I wore a tux to match. The white gardenias in her hair matched the ones in her bouquet.

Susan's father officiated, beaming along with the sun. As he took our hands in his just before the final blessing, though, his expression changed; he began to tremble. Somehow he managed to maintain his composure for the rest of the ceremony.

With her mother's help, Susan catered much of our wedding reception. Over 300 guests flocked to our celebration.

After a honeymoon on beautiful Kiawah Island off the South Carolina coast, we headed back to our small apartment. I already liked being married, and knew I was going to be one happy man.

We'd been back in Greensboro for only a few hours when the phone rang.

"Hi, Rob," my cousin Art said. "I'm sorry to bother you this soon. But I've got some bad news."

He paused; my heart sank.

I could guess the reason for his call. Four months had passed since Susan and I had been to Chicago. That visit and subsequent updates had prepared me for what I was about to hear. I motioned for Susan to listen with me.

"Gigi died on Monday. I didn't want to call you on your honeymoon, and didn't know when you would be back. So I just started calling this number yesterday."

I tried to stay focused. "Can you give me the details?"

"I was with Gigi on your wedding day. That afternoon she kept asking me when you were getting married. Each time I told her, 'Today, Gigi, he and Susan are getting married today.'

"Once she finally understood that it truly was the day you were getting married, she went to sleep and never regained consciousness. I stayed in Chicago until she died."

"Thanks, Art. You've been so good to her. I'm sorry I wasn't there to be with her, too."

"I know how hard this is for you, Rob," Art said gently. "She loved you very much. The doctors said there was no medical reason she should have lived this long. She was proud of you when you graduated from college. But she still worried about you being alone. On the day you were married, she passed you into Susan's hands. She liked your new wife, you know."

"Yes, Art, I know," I managed to reply. "She always promised she would see me graduate from college and get married."

"I feel certain she somehow willed herself to survive until your wedding."

I couldn't speak.

He went on to describe Gigi's final arrangements. I thanked him for all his kindness to me, and especially for the care he'd shown Gigi.

When I hung up, Susan watched and waited.

"Let's go for a ride," I said, heading for the door. "You drive."

My bride drove with tear-filled eyes as I silently sat beside her in the little Volkswagen.

Wrapping my arms around myself with hands tucked into armpits, I began to rock slightly side to side—much as I had so many years before when, through blurry, little-boy eyes, I'd watched my Gigi walk away.

Each time I'd wondered whether she would come back. This time she wouldn't.

This simple, poor, but godly woman had loved me more than her own life. She'd given me all she had, and now she was gone.

No longer could I call her on Sunday afternoons, or enjoy her Boston pot roast. No longer could I tell her how much I loved her.

The finality crushed me.

We drove for about 20 minutes before Susan sensed the impending eruption. As soon as she pulled into a deserted parking lot, I exploded into anguished sobs.

The little car shook as I rocked back and forth, groaning with sorrow too deep for words. Saying nothing, Susan held me close, crying with me and for me.

It was nearly 30 minutes later when we finally collapsed against the seat in exhaustion, unable to shed another tear.

Then God and Susan took me to a place I'd always wanted to be.

Home.

Epilogue

Twenty years after Gigi died, I was cleaning old boxes from my attic. I found her little spiral-bound journal, and the following entry:

> *Robby, darling—*
>
> *You are my precious grandson. I hope you will grow up to be strong physically, spiritually, and mentally; that you will be a good citizen and strong enough to protect the things in which you believe.*
>
> *Always keep love in your heart—you will always have my love.*
>
> *—Grandmother Gigi*

I also found this brief description of the time Mother abducted me:

> *Christmas of 1962 and first months of 1963 were unpleasant for Robby and me but by summer 1963 we had things under control.*

Gigi's prayer for my future and her matter-of-fact way of dealing with the chaos in my life may help to explain some of how I got where I am today.

I've outlived the orphanage where I grew up. In the winter of 2005, the Covenant Children's Home was torn down. The place that housed so many castaway kids is physically gone.

Fortunately, I live in a home that can never be demolished—my relationship with my heavenly Father. And I'm looking forward to another everlasting home. As the Bible says in 2 Corinthians 5:1, "For we know that if the earthly tent which is our house is torn down, we have a building from God, a house not made with hands, eternal in the heavens."

Susan and I recently celebrated 26 years of faithful marriage. After 22 years as a homemaker, she's pursuing her masters of divinity degree. Like most couples, we've had times that were wonderfully fulfilling and periods of great stress. I'm happy to report that we still love each other—and that this hound still chases her around the house.

We have two neat kids. Alicia finished college in three years with a degree in Christian education, graduating *cum laude.* She married a fine young man, Chad, who is headed to law school.

Our son, Luke, is 19 at this writing. He's studying the music industry, leaning toward using his scholarship-winning voice and ability to play multiple instruments in some kind of Christian ministry.

When Alicia and Luke became mature enough, we shared parts of my childhood with them. We also took them to Princeton to see the Home. I celebrate the fact that they'll never come close to understanding what I went through.

Susan and I also celebrate that our kids have chosen the faith of their parents—and live it fully and genuinely.

In 1985 I became a financial consultant. Business has brought successes and failures, but in 2002 a leading magazine of the industry recognized me as one of America's outstanding brokers.

I've kept my promise to Tony Martin, the Children's Home gardener, by never forgetting the "little guy." Many of my clients are wealthy, but I still don't turn away the "small" investor.

My father died in 1983, three years after Susan and I married. There was a funeral for immediate family; burial was on a cold, wet, windy day with Aunt Alice, Uncle Mack, their three children, and a couple of my father's cousins in attendance.

I chose a closed-casket service, so my father's photo is still the only picture of him that I carry in my mind. We still use some of the heirloom furniture that caused him so much anguish, as well as the crystal, china, and silver.

I stay in touch with many people from my past. Uncle Mack and all of my great-uncles have died, but at this writing I talk and visit with Aunt Alice and Mack, Jr. Art still lives in Rockford.

A couple of times a year I check in with Nola, who retired and married later in life. Paul, my fellow "inmate," is like a brother. I also stay in touch with Marv, Dave, and Swaney as well as my missionary friends. Recently I reconnected with my counselor John, but unfortunately lost all contact with my African friend, Dapala.

Often, after hearing parts of my story, people ask, "How did you survive and become the person you are today?"

The answers are complex, but the foundational truth isn't: I couldn't change the events and circumstances imposed on me, but I could choose how to respond. The mark of a person, it seems to me, is not just in how one acts but also in how one reacts.

Society said I was just a kid from an orphanage, probably doomed to a life of meaningless drifting, an early death, or prison. Genetics suggested I might suffer my parents' afflictions. I chose to change my vision of who I was and who I could become. Caring adults tried to reach me, but ultimately I had to reach back to them and upward toward God.

When I reached out to God for the hope offered everyone

regardless of race, language, or culture, I learned that nothing I do to myself or is done to me by others, no abuse or apathy, nothing that has happened or ever will happen—including death—can separate me from the love of God. That love helped me to forgive, releasing me from my painful past—just as that love has helped so many others forgive and find freedom.

My goal in sharing this story isn't just to bring hope to other castaway kids. It's to remind you that your life matters.

There's always hope when you find the home where you're not a guest. I sincerely believe that kind of home is found by choosing to have a personal relationship with God and fellowship with people who also have chosen such a relationship.

For me, that began with a simple, sincere prayer: *Jesus, if You are real, come into my nightmare. Forgive me of my sins and change me.*

As you hopefully face the issues of your past, deal with the realities of your present, and look toward your future, may you find answers. May the choices you make allow us to say together what was said so well by the former Saul of Tarsus:

> *I am still not all I should be but I am bringing all my energies to bear on this one thing: Forgetting the past and looking forward to what lies ahead.*
>
> —PHILIPPIANS 3:13, TLB

A Note to Educators

Teachers are often encouraged to make sure other voices and cultures are part of the curriculum. The true voice of an abandoned kid who was one of the last "lifers" in an American orphanage might qualify as a different voice and culture.

Here's what a 25-year veteran high school English teacher had to say about this story after her seven twelfth-grade classes read a draft copy of *Castaway Kid*:

"This is an amazing work of contemporary literature that explores universal themes of loneliness, rejection, anger, bitterness, and the need for forgiveness. I was surprised by the wide range of different responses and especially how honestly the boys responded and became fully engaged."

Equally telling are these high school students' responses to the manuscript:

"Couldn't put it down. Your open-ended questions really made me think."

"Many chapter endings were dramatic cliff-hangers. I experienced the struggles with you, loved the romantic stuff with your future wife, laughed out loud as I related to being a dork with girls."

"This wasn't just hope for kids like you but for all of us."

"It is an incredible story, amazing adventures."

"Fresh."

"Really liked how you got me inside your head, appreciated

being with you in the struggle to forgive—and the fact that you didn't make what is really hard seem as if it's easy."

If you're an educator in English, literature, sociology, psychology, or juvenile justice, I hope you'll consider using this true story as an optional reading assignment. I stand side by side with you in trying to help students become all they can be.

—*R.B. Mitchell*

For Further Reading

This book contains many references to other literary works, including the Bible. If you'd like to explore them further, here's a list of these references and the sources from which they're drawn.

Chapter 4

"It was my turn to cry out with groanings too deep for words." See the Bible, Romans 8:26.

Chapter 8

"I'll try to do and be anything you want, if you'll only keep me." *Anne of Green Gables* by L. M. Montgomery (Bantam Books, 1998), p. 47.

Chapter 9

"This reminds me of *Oliver Twist.*" See *Oliver Twist* by Charles Dickens (Barnes & Noble Classics, 2003), p. 38.

Chapter 12

"Around that time I read *Up from Slavery* by Booker T. Washington, the slave turned educator." See *Up from Slavery* by Booker T. Washington (Signet Classics, 2000).

Chapter 14

"One day I asked him, 'How can someone believe in a hope they can't see?' " See the Bible, Hebrews 11:1.

Chapter 18

"This guy got hungry, thirsty, and tired. He even got His feet dirty." See the Bible, Mark 11:12; John 19:28; Mark 6:31; John 13:3-17.

"He was let down by those He trusted." See the Bible, Mark 14:43-46.

"Then I read a verse that knocked my socks off. *This man said He is God. . . .*

"Apparently that claim was so offensive to the religious leaders of the day that they set up a plan to have Him killed." See the Bible, John 8:51-59.

"Either Jesus was a lunatic or lied about being God—or was really who He claimed to be." See *Mere Christianity* by C. S. Lewis (Touchstone, 1996), p. 56.

"It surprised me that Jesus got angry." See the Bible, Mark 3:5.

"We both got angry at hypocrisy; I liked that." See the Bible, Matthew 23:13-33.

"He got frustrated at people; so did I." See the Bible, Mark 3:5.

"I saw that Jesus talked often about eternal life. I was more worried about living past 20." See the Bible, John 3:16-17.

"Jesus said the Spirit of God could come into my heart and change me. *How can something like the Spirit of God fit into my body, into my heart? How can I believe in something I can't see or touch?"* See the Bible, John 3:1-15.

"I kept reading, noting that Jesus said thieves come to steal, kill, and destroy—while He came so we can have 'abundant' life." See the Bible, John 10:10.

"When I got to Bible sections about Jesus healing the crippled, blind, and deaf, I usually passed them over." See the Bible, Matthew 11:1-6.

"Tell me, Robby, how do you explain the guys who ran closest to Jesus and then watched Him die on the cross? They buried His body and then claimed to have seen Him rise from that grave, just like He promised." See the Bible, Matthew 27–28; John 19–21; Hebrews 11:35–12:2.

"Did you read about the more than 500 who claimed they saw Him after He rose from the grave?" See the Bible, 1 Corinthians 15:1-8.

"I know if a kid disobeys his parent, that kid should apologize and ask for forgiveness." See the Bible, Ephesians 6:1.

"Something was trying to open the locked doors of my heart." See the Bible, Revelation 3:20.

"What am I going to decide about this Jesus? Am I going to reject Him as a lunatic like my mother, or risk reaching out one more time for hope and accept Him as who He says He is?" See the Bible, Matthew 16:13-17.

Chapter 19

"As with Ralph and Jack at Castle Rock in *Lord of the Flies,* someone was gonna get hurt." See *Lord of the Flies* by William Golding (Perigee, 1976), p. 169.

"Suddenly, though, I remembered the words of Jesus: 'Turn the other cheek.'" See the Bible, Matthew 5:39.

"I flipped the book over. Then I read a verse: 'A gentle answer turns away wrath.' " The Bible, Proverbs 15:1.

"Looking for encouragement, I returned to reading Booker T. Washington's *Up from Slavery.* One of the statements I saw there was, 'The Negro youth starts out with the presumption against him.' " *Up from Slavery* by Booker T. Washington (Signet Classics, 2000), p. 25.

Chapter 21

"And now, 'Just as I Am,' the God of the universe was offering to adopt me." See the Bible, Romans 8:14-17.

Chapter 23

"Suddenly . . . I found my right fist closing, tensing. I heard the sound of flies buzzing. The 'old me' rose like a lion who'd been lying camouflaged in the grass.

"A familiar voice that only I could hear seemed to be laughing at me, coming from just inside the jungle that lined the soccer field. *Smash his face in! Hit, hit, hit, and he'll be down before he knows it and hurting for a week!*

"You can't escape your past. Do it! Do it now!"

See *Lord of the Flies* by William Golding (Perigee, 1976), pp. 136, 143-144.

"Turn the other cheek and walk away." See the Bible, Matthew 5:39.

Chapter 24

"But then I heard the story of Corrie ten Boom." See *The Hiding Place* by Corrie ten Boom, Elizabeth Sherrill, and John Sherrill (Chosen Books, 2006).

Chapter 26

"The two of them must have seemed like the tormenting harpies I'd read about in Dante's *Inferno*; my father couldn't find a way to free himself from their claws and constant pecking." See *Inferno* by Dante Alighieri (Signet Classics, 2001), pp. 118, 124), believed first published around 1341. In Canto XIII, Dante is led into what is referred to as the Second Ring of the Seventh Circle of Hell, a place for those who were violent against themselves. There they are constantly tormented by harpies.

Chapter 27

"The fifth of the Ten Commandments, 'Honor your father and your mother,' kept bothering me." The Bible, Exodus 20:12.

"There I read, 'Casting all your anxiety on Him, because He cares for you.' " The Bible, 1 Peter 5:7.

"For the next week, a calm guarded my heart and mind." See the Bible, Philippians 4:7.

"Having chosen not to be a victim crippled by childhood trauma, I felt free—as if heavy chains had been removed from my legs." See the Bible, Galatians 5:1.

Epilogue

"When I reached out to God for the hope offered everyone regardless of race, language, or culture, I learned that nothing I do to myself or is done to me by others, no abuse or apathy, nothing that has happened or ever will happen—including death—can separate me from the love of God." See the Bible, Romans 8:38-39.